The Americans
The Illustrative Story of a Hand Balancer
...from Mexico to Colombia to Santa Monica, California

2nd Revised Edition
By Author
David Darseli Santana

Analytical Evaluation by
Marcos Ignacio Santana

All Images and Content © Darseli Book Publishing, David Darseli Santana. All Rights Reserved
Darseli Book Publishing, Santa Monica, California
2nd Rev. Ed. Book Publication In English: July 3, 2022

All text and Images Copyright Darseli Book Publiing, David Darseli Santana. All Rights Reserved. No part of this book may be reproduced, stored in a retrieval system, or transmitted in any form or by any means, electronic, mechanical, photocopying, recording, the Internet, or otherwise without the legal expressed written notarized permission of the copyright owner.
Legal Counsel for Darseli Book Publishing and David Darseli Santana:
Law Office of Dinah Perez, P.C., 1801 Century Park East, Suite 2400, Los Angeles, CA 90067

(C) 2022 Darseli Book Publishing. David Darseli Santana. All Rights Reserved.
The Americans ...The Illustrative Story of a Hand Balancer...from Mexico to Colombia to Santa Monica, California 2nd Revised Edition By Author David Darseli Santana, Analystical Evaluation By Marcos Ignacio Santana
ISBN: **978-1-955535-04-5.** Publisher Identification Serial Number:2022DBPAMERICANS1968MARCH7ENGLISH-PF

Referencing Keywords: 1. Acrobatics 2. Hand Balancing -Technique 3. Acrobatic Adventure 4.Title, 5 Colombia, 6. Santa Monica, California, 7. Panama, 8. Mexico, 9. Nicaragua, 10. Guatemala 11) Muscle Beach, 12) Ringling Brother and Barnum And Baily Circus.

Book Order requests of 10 or more can be made directly to the Publisher. Contact and Order information can be provided by emailing a request to: DarseliBookPublishing@ProtonMail.Com. Correspondence Attention: Orlando Quiroga Torres.

This published book copy is a Publisher Copy. All book copies of this title are exclusive property of Publisher (Darseli Book Publishing). Access to this book and any DBP book and their respective "mediums" copies is by License ONLY. In order to obtain access to this title, you must agree with the **End User License Agreement (also known as EULA)** found in the page and the following 2 pages (and in Publisher official websites). Upon acceptance of this **EULA**, and the purchase of a license, you can obtain access to this DBP intellectual property.

Please carefully read this page and the following 2 **EULA** pages>>> to understand how to obtain access to a Publisher copy of this intellectual property (**an updatable EULA** can be found on Publisher website **Darseli.Com OR by request at: DarseliBookPublishing@ProtonMail.Com). ALSO: UPON REQUEST, A LARGER FONT SIZE OF THIS EULA AGREEMENT CAN BE EMAILED TO YOU. PLEASE REQUEST AT:** DarseliBookPublishing@ProtonMail.Com.

1

EULA SECTION ILA (Sec. 1 of 9): Introduction Agreement To License:
ILA 1: Darseli Book Publishing is hereinbefore and hereinhere and hereinafter referred to as, but not limited to: Publisher, us, our, DBP, Darseli Book Publishing, Grantor, intellectual property owner, author, Licensor, or similar references.
ILA 2: You the potential license buyer or purchaser or non-purchaser of the License to access the DBP product or book and its corresponding Publisher Owned "Medium" in this license agreement is referred to but not limited to: "I", the licensee, purchaser, you, your, and similar references.
ILA 3: By purchasing a license to access the DBP product or book (licensed intellectual property) listed above (or any DBP product) and its corresponding "Medium" you FULLY agree to the terms and conditions of this license agreement INCLUDING, WITHOUT LIMITATION, THE PROVISIONS ON LICENSE RESTRICTION, which began above and continues below. By your full agreement of this EULA you may purchase a license to come into access of a specified DBP product or book and its corresponding "Medium" (Medium owned perpetually by the Publisher).
ILA 4: Hereinbefore and hereinhere and hereinafter, the DBP product's or book's "Medium" refers to the medium used to house or place the intellectual property on such as but not limited to: paper medium, electronic medium, and so forth. If you came upon the book or its corresponding "Medium" without the purchase of a license, you are not authorize to use this intellectual property and its corresponding "Medium" which is property of the Publisher at all times and places. That is, the "Medium" (as well as the book or DBP product) remains at all times and places exclusive property of the Publisher. Accordingly, you Understand and Agree that this book and its "Medium" is NOT for SALE. The License purchased only grants you access to the book and its corresponding "Medium" in accordance to this EULA which describes among other items the restrictions of use of the book or DBP product and its corresponding "Medium".
ILA 5: You understand and agree that If you purchased the license to access a DBP product or book (intellectual property) and its corresponding "medium" format (paper or otherwise) and do not agree with the terms of this license agreement (EULA) after rereading them, return the intellectual property and its "Medium" within 34 days for a full LICENSE FEE refund (subject to DBP's Return Policy Found at Darseli.Com) TO THE PLACE WHERE YOU OBTAINED IT (be it either from the Publisher OR ITS AUTHORIZED AGENT (current DBP Authorized Agents listed at Darseli.Com, or by emailing us and requesting the current DBP Authorized Agents list to: MiCostaBella@Gmail.Com).
The DBP product or book and its corresponding "medium" MUST BE RETURNED at the time of refund request, and our authorization to do so, AND BEFORE REFUND in order to receive a LICENSE FEE refund. Shipping expense for the return of the licensed book and its "Medium" is at your expense if shipping is necessary. After the 34 days, NO REFUND of license fee is granted even if the Publisher terminates your license to use the book (DBP product) and its corresponding "Medium" for any reason including violation of this license agreement or suspected violation of this license agreement or for any other reason or for no reason.Additionally, you understand and agree to re-read and FULLY agree to the full elaborate complete, and up to date EULA found at www.Darseli.Com, or by requesting the full current DBP EULA at MiCostaBella@Gmail.Com within 20 days of license purchase.
ILA 6-Sub 1: Full refund applies only to "PAPER" medium format or similar Tangible "Medium" format of the book (DBP product). Intangible format of the book (such as electronic "Medium" format of the book and similar) are NOT entitled for refund even if your license to use the book is terminated by Publisher for violation or suspected violation of the book license agreement or for any reason or no reason, or by your disagreement with the full book license agreement (EULA).
ILA 6-Sub 2: Accordingly, for such intangible "Medium" format such as "electronic" format (and tangible "Medium" formats such as "paper"), the Publisher STRONGLY advises the potential purchaser of a DBP license to CAREFULLY read the license agreement in full, understand it completely, and FULLY agree with it completely BEFORE purchasing a DBP license to access any DBP product and its corresponding "medium".
ILA 7: This is an agreement made between you, the entity in possession or to be in possession of our intellectual property and its corresponding "Medium" via the purchase of a license or the license purchaser or potential purchaser of the license or entity in possession of our book and its "Medium" (irrespective of being authorized or not) AND the Publisher of the DBP product or book.
ILA 8: An entity may not purchase a license to access the DBP product or book and its corresponding medium if the entity is not considered a legal adult in their country of origin where they are a citizen. Minors living under the same physical residence of the legal adult purchaser of a DBP license, may access the DBP product or book and its corresponding "Medium" for personal use only and as outlined in this license agreement. The minor must be supervised at all times by the DBP license purchaser when using any DBP product including books and their corresponding medium. And the DBP license purchaser is responsible for the acts of the minor that go against the interest of the Publisher and its intellectual property and corresponding mediums and the EULA. You fully agree that Any violation by the minor against this EULA makes the purchaser of a DBP license and its corresponding medium fully liable. Purchaser is the DBP license buyer granted access to the DBP product or the book and its corresponding "Medium". The purchaser is also the entity that has agreed to this EULA and proceeded to purchase a DBP license to access the Publisher's intellectual property and its corresponding medium.
ILA 9: This license agreement to access the DBP product and its corresponding "Medium" is NOT a contract for sale and or rent of a DBP product or book or its corresponding "Medium": RATHER, it is a license to access and use a DBP product or book and its corresponding "Medium" subject to the terms and conditions of this Agreement (EULA). The DBP product or book and its corresponding "Medium" is licensed NOT SOLD.
ILA 10: You fully agree that The DBP product or book and its corresponding "Medium" (physical or non-physical) (in paper, plastic, electronic format, or otherwise) is always property of the Publisher and cannot be transferred by the licensee or third party or any other entity at anytime or place. You also understand and fully agree that the DBP product or book and its corresponding "Medium" provided is Not for you to give-away, sale, rent, license, sublicense, transfer, delegate, or otherwise at any time and at any location by you or a third party or any entity be it at a physical place, the Internet or otherwise (said items always remain exclusive property of the Publisher). You also fully agree that You are only granted a license to access and use the intellectual property and its "Medium" for personal use only and as to the terms of this agreement.
ILA 11: Please read the terms and conditions above and below carefully.
DBP and you agree on the above and the below sections and everything in it. If you do not FULLY agree with this EULA, you may not purchase a license to use any DBP product or book and its corresponding "Medium" or maintain the book and its corresponding "medium" in your possession. Furthermore, No entity may have in its/his/her possession any DBP product or book and its corresponding "Medium" without having a purchased Publisher granted license to access them unless otherwise stated in this EULA.
EULA SECTION NTI (Sec. 2 of 9):: Non-Transferable Disclosure (NTD)
NTD 1: You may have an additional notarized written agreement directly with Publisher (for example: a volume license agreement) that only supplements this agreement. You agree that In no way does any other written agreement with the Publisher contradict the core of this license agreement including the understanding that the publisher maintains at all times and places exclusive ownership of the DBP product or book and its corresponding "Medium", and you agree that the license restrictions and all other restrictions in this license agreement (EULA) are preserved in any other additional written agreement that may be made by the Publisher and you or other entity (including an entity that is granted status by the Publisher as an Authorized Agent of the Publisher).
NTD 2: Limited Rights. Upon payment of the nonrefundable DBP license fee (refundable only within 34 days as stated earlier for paper "medium" format only), you agree that DBP grants you a limited, non-exclusive, revocable, nontransferable license to use a particular respective DBP product or book (intellectual property) and its corresponding "Medium". You agree that any authorized agent granted by the Publisher must follow the core outline of this EULA as well at all times.
EULA SECTION NDPA (Sec. 3 of 9): No Distribution Permitted Agreement (NDPA):
NDPA 1: This Agreement describes the terms governing your use of the DBP product or book (intellectual property), intellectual property content, and the corresponding "Medium" in any format.
NDPA 2A: You and any other entity further and additionally FULLY agree, understand, and accept that the United States (U.S.) Copyright Law SECTION § 109, and also in particular its (§ 109) subsection (a) and (c) (or any other nation similar section) do not apply to this agreement or any DBP product; and you and any other entity who may be in possession of a DBP product or the book and or its corresponding "Medium" understand and agree not to use this said Copyright section to contradict this EULA, since this DBP product or book and its corresponding "Medium" are licensed and not sold.
NDPA 2B: Furthermore, you agree that as to this section, and subsection (d), of aforementioned U.S. Copyright Law, you are not permitted to post or sale or give-away or otherwise on the Internet or any other medium of communication or platform, or anywhere or place any DBP product and its "medium" without the exclusive notarized written authorization of the copyright owner and Publisher. That is, as to this EULA and its corresponding DBP product or book and its "Medium", The privileges prescribed by subsections (a) and (c) and (d) [of U.S. Copyright Section §109] do not apply to any DBP product and its "Mediums" since DBP products are licensed Not Sold and your privileges to access our DBP products and books and its "Medium" are limited as described in this EULA.
NDPA 3A: You understand and agree that the granted license, DBP products or this book, and its corresponding "Medium" CANNOT, at no time or place, by you or any other entity (besides the Publisher and a specified notarized authorized DBP Agent) be leased, licensed, sub-licensed, loaned, assign, conveyed, transferred, copied, reproduced, modified, adapted, merged, translated, given-away, rented, displayed and or announced to the public in any platform or way, or sold or otherwise distributed in any way, shape, form or format by you or any entity other than the Publisher and its specified notarized authorized DBP Agent, or as specified in this EULA.
You agree that Only the Publisher and the Publisher's designated Publisher Authorized Agents of any DBP product may provide distribution of "license" of DBP products or this book and its corresponding "Medium" in accordance to this license agreement.
NDPA 3B: PROPRIETARY RIGHTS: Except where specifically stated otherwise in this EULA, you understand and agree that DBP owns all rights, titles and interest in and to all DBP products and their corresponding Medium including, without limitation, all intellectual and proprietary rights appurtenant thereto, and, except for the limited license granted to you herein, nothing in this EULA shall be construed to transfer, convey, impair or otherwise adversely affect DBP and its authors et al. ownership or proprietary rights therein or any other DBP information or materials, tangible or intangible, in any form and in any medium. All intellectual property rights, including copyright, patents, trademarks and trade secrets, are retained by the Publisher and its affiliates, licensors, and collaborators, all rights reserved.
You understand and agree that you may not copy, imitate or use the Trademarks et al., in whole or in part, for any purpose. No license or other right to use any Trademark et al. used or displayed on any of our mediums or marketing material is granted to You.
NDPA 3C: You understand and agree that **you may always view the Current List of Authorized Agents of DBP on its website or you can request a Current list at: MiCostaBella@Gmail.Com.** You further understand and agree that you will check the Current list of authorized Agents of DBP, before purchasing a DBP license, to make sure you are buying your license legally before you purchase any DBP license to access any DBP product and its corresponding medium.
NDPA 4-sub 1: You understand and agree and will honor that Darseli Book Publishing holds exclusive distribution rights of its products and corresponding mediums on any platform, the INTERNET or other electronic market places or similar electronic devises in addition to all non-Internet platforms.
You understand and agree that An editorial review or other similar opinion may reference the intellectual property in an article or news feed only so far as it does not imply any monetary gain for entity providing such news feed or book review article. Written request to do so can be made to the Publisher at: MiCostaBella@Gmail.Com. The exception would be a notarized written agreement with the Publisher in advance.
NDPA 4-sub 2: You understand and agree that All authorized license distribution Authorized Agent entities must agree with DBP on a Separate notarized written Agreement before the distribution entity is authorized to distribute any DBP license (including the DBP product's corresponding Publisher's medium {physical or non-physical cover and pages in paper format and/or electronic format, or otherwise containing a particular DBP product}) on behalf of the Publisher, and only after the granted distribution agent entity is on the "CURRENT AND UP-TO-DATE" DBP Authorized Agent List posted at Darseli.com website or by request of current agent list to MiCostaBella@Gmail.Com. This Agent List fluctuates (CHANGES) and so it is recommended to check the Updated Authorized DBP Agent List as indicated BEFORE DEALING WITH an apparent Publisher Authorized Agent or to make sure you are dealing with a Current and Valid Publisher Authorized Agent. Publisher Authorized License Reseller can be terminated by the Publisher at any time for any reason, especially in a violation of this EULA or its agreed commitments to DBP and general business integrity and ethical standards.
LGR 1-sub-1: YOU agree you will Not Transfer your license, lease or sublease your license, rent or license or sublicense your license, sale your license, assign your license, delegate or transfer or give-away your license rights of any DBP product, book (or e-book),or its Publisher owned "Medium" in any way or format or time or place (or in any format that may be conceived now or in the future). That is, you understand and agree that this limited DBP license is granted to you and you alone (license is exclusive to you only).

LGR 1-sub-2: YOU agree you will Not authorize another individual or entity to copy, reproduce, modify, adapt, merge, translate, assign, transfer or otherwise any DBP product or book and its corresponding "Medium" onto any computer or any other platform.

LGR 1-sub-3: You further agree and understand that the license granted to you pertains to only one corresponding DBP product and its corresponding "Medium" and no more. If you wish to purchase an additional license to have access to another single corresponding DBP product or book (and its "Medium"), you understand and agree that you must purchase another (separate) license to do so (allowing you access to that license's single corresponding book and DBP product and its corresponding "Medium").

LGR 2-sub-1: The book or DBP product is licensed to you generally for the "life" of the corresponding physical or electronic, or otherwise "Medium" or as to a specified time given by the Publisher at the time of ordering or acquiring from the Publisher or Publisher's authorized agent (so long as you abide by the EULA) as to this EULA or immediately terminate access if Publisher decides to revoke your license (and access to its corresponding DBP product and Medium) for any reason.

LGR 2-sub-2: You understand and agree that this license is revocable and can be Terminated by the Publisher at any time for any reason and without notice to you. Reason for termination may include your violation of this agreement or suspected violation of this agreement. At such time, you agree to surrender the book and its "Medium" (which is property of the Publisher at all times and places) to the Publisher or immediately destroy it if Publisher asks you to do so.

LGR 2-sub-3: You understand and agree that if you are No Longer interested in the DBP product or book during the period specified in the granted DBP product license, you acknowledge and agree that you will destroy the book and its corresponding "Medium" (or if e-Book or similar "Medium" format: delete the electronic file or similar file of the DBP product and its corresponding "Medium" provided).

LGR2-sub-4: You understand and agree that a DBP license purchaser can obtain their unique DBP license number by adding in sequence the unique DBP license serial number components using the following DBP license identifiers:

(1) The word or symbol "DBP" at   beginning,
(2) followed by the YEAR, MONTH,   DAY of DBP License purchase date,
(3) followed by one Family Name of   DBP product license Purchaser,
(4) followed by the number of DBP   licenses ordered in numerical digits (2 or more licenses listed as A1, B1, C1,... Ax, Bx, Cx,etc.)
(5) The DBP license Purchaser's   Country of Origin as indicated,
(6) followed by the numerical date: 4-13-1950,
(7) and followed by and ended with the first (non-article) Word in the title of the corresponding DBP product.

You further agree that if the Publisher asks for this DBP license number, you will furnish it to the Publisher as an authentication of your DBP product license purchase. Accordingly, you agree to write this DBP product license number somewhere secure where you can access it if need be. **You also understand and agree that we may ask, and you will provide, additional identifiers to verify that you are the actual purchaser of the DBP product license.**

LGR 3: You agree that you are never allowed to obtain any tangible or intangible monetary or similar benefits for sharing unless otherwise specified in this EULA.

LGR 4: You further understand and agree that Only the Publisher or the Publisher's Authorized Agents (current authorized agents posted on the current DBP list at Darseli. Com or by request at MiCostaBella@Gmail.Com) are allowed to distribute a DBP product license, the DBP product and its corresponding license-only Publisher "Medium" which belongs to Publisher at all times and places.

LGR 5: Non-Profit public libraries (herein herewith also known as "public library" or "public libraries" or "library" or "libraries") are the ONLY ENTITY permitted in this license agreement to allow their patrons to check out "share" the book and its "medium", FREE OF CHARGE, as a form of sharing the book so long as the book is returned to the original licensed entity (the public library that purchased a corresponding license to a single corresponding book from the Publisher).

LGR 5 sub-1: Aforementioned Libraries CANNOT sell, lease, sublease, license, sub-license, give away, rent, rent for monetary gain, copy, reproduce, modify, adapt, or otherwise the License, the book or DBP product, and its corresponding "Medium" at ANYTIME for any reason including if the public library decides to discard the book and its "Medium": in such cases the book (or DBP product) and its corresponding "Medium" must be destroyed by the library holding a corresponding DBP license, or return, at its expense, to the Publisher the DBP product and its corresponding Medium. If the said medium is in electronic or similar format, the library agrees to delete or otherwise destroy the DBP product's licensed medium.

LGR 7 sub-2A: All other restrictions in this DBP product license agreement apply directly to public libraries as well. If the public library does not agree fully with this EULA or any part of this agreement, they are not permitted to purchase a license of a DBP product or book or to acquire (by any means) a DBP product or the book and its corresponding "Medium".

LGR 8: EDUCATOR PRIVILEGES as to a DBP license: A credentialed, certificated educator may share the book or DBP product and its corresponding medium with his or her assigned students during school hours within the school on-site physical classroom. Students must be supervised at all time by the DBP license purchaser (educator) when using any DBP product including books and their corresponding medium. Students may not borrow the book as it is to remain with the educator (who purchased the DBP product license) at all times. And said DBP license purchaser is responsible for the acts of the students that go against the interest of the Publisher and its intellectual property and corresponding mediums and the EULA. The "Educator" DBP license purchaser understands and agrees that Any violation by students against this EULA makes the "EDUCATOR" purchaser of a DBP license fully liable.

LGR 9: The DBP product License does not allow the DBP product to be used on more than one "Medium" other than that provided to you by the Publisher or its authorized agent at time of license purchase, and you understand and agree that you may not make the book or DBP product available over additional physical "Medium" formats or electronic "Medium" formats or any other type of "Medium" formats or any type of network where it could be used by multiple people or devices or multiple computers at the same time or stand-alone. This DBP product License does not grant you any rights to share the DBP issued license, the book or DBP product and its corresponding "Medium" other than those explicitly stated in this Agreement.

EULA SECTION T (Sec. 5 of 9): Termination (T1)

T1: The Publisher, Darseli Book Publishing, may, at its sole discretion and without notice, terminate your DBP product license for ANY REASON effective immediately. Such license termination by the Publisher terminates your access to use the single corresponding DBP product and its corresponding "Medium" (Medium owned by the Publisher at all times and places). Upon Termination stated, you understand and agree that you are not entitled to any compensation or refund of any kind due to said termination or otherwise. You also agree that Upon termination of your license by Publisher you must immediately stop using the book or DBP product and its "Medium" and destroy the DBP product and its corresponding "Medium", or return them to the Publisher (at your own shipping expense). If the book or DBP product and its "Medium" is in digital format or similar format, then you are instructed to immediately delete the DBP product and its corresponding "medium" from your hard drive or other storage mechanism or constructs or otherwise upon termination of your license.

T2: If in turn you wish to terminate (end) an issued license and this license agreement of a DBP product or book (such termination by you effectively and immediately terminates your access to the book or DBP product and its corresponding "Medium"), you must immediately destroy or return (at your own shipping expense) to Publisher the book and its "Medium" as described above. The balance of the Agreement shall survive any such 'termination of license rights'. You are not entitled to a license fee refund upon termination unless specified differently in this license agreement.

EULA SECTION LPMA (Sec. 6 of 9): License Fee Payment And Modification Agreement (LPMA):

LPMA 1: You agree and understand that the DBP product license to be issued to you (and possession of its single corresponding book and its Publisher's "medium"), upon and after your agreement of this EULA license agreement, requires payment to the Publisher or its authorized agent at the current set "License Fee" amount, or license fee amount presented to you, for the completion of a DBP product license issuance to you.

LPMA 2: Certain book or DBP product license issuances by Publisher to particular individuals or organizations are granted without a license fee for the sole purpose of promotional review of the book and its "Medium". Such granted DBP product licenses to these particular individuals or organizations by the Publisher are also bound to this license agreement and its sections in its entirety (which includes non-transferable rules of the license, the book or its Publisher owned "Medium" or selling of book or DBP product or otherwise transferring DBP products in violation of this DBP product license agreement). If aforementioned particular entity receiving from the Publisher such a DBP product license with its corresponding book and its "medium" in this way does not fully agree with this EULA license agreement, then their granted license is immediately revoked and they agree that they must immediately return (at their shipping expense) or destroy their provided licensed DBP product and its corresponding "Medium", and all other parts of this license agreement survive.

LPMA 3: You understand and agree that The Publisher reserves the right to modify this agreement (EULA) at any time to reflect, for example but not limited to, and without notice, changes in our business or to maintain a DBP product or book in a license ONLY format. If DBP modifies this EULA agreement a revised version will be posted on our website www.darseli.com and/or our official social web pages or you may request the current EULA by email to: MiCostaBella@Gmail.Com. You agree that your continued use of any of our DBP products and books and their corresponding "Medium" will constitute your acceptance of the modified agreement that can be made at any time and without notice other than posting a revised agreement on one of our official web pages or our other public notice platforms at our option or by you requesting a revised EULA via email as stated. If you do not agree with the DBP revised license agreement (EULA) changes allowing you to have continued access to any of our DBP products or books and their respective corresponding "Medium" in your possession or to be in your possession, you herewith agree to destroy or return the DBP product and its corresponding "Medium" (shipping expense belongs to you) to the Publisher (or its authorized agent) without a refund or any other sort of compensation to you.

EULA SECTION LLLA (Sec. 7 of 9): Language and Law Of License Agreement (LLLA):

LLLA 1: The controlling language of this agreement is in English ONLY. Any translation of this license agreement to any other language besides English that you may have received is provided only for your convenience. You understand and agree If any discrepancies are found in language translation of this EULA, the controlling language of this EULA is English always.

LLLA 2A: Controlling Law and Severability: This license is to be governed by the State of Washington, U.S.A. If any part of this agreement is found void and unenforceable by a legitimate government entity court, it will not affect the validity of the balance of this agreement, which will remain valid and enforceable according to its terms. This agreement may only be modified in writing by the Publisher: Darseli Book Publishing (DBP). Again, the English version of this agreement will be the ONLY version used when interpreting or construing this agreement.

LLLA 2B: You irrevocably and unconditionally (a) consent to submit to the exclusive jurisdiction of the state and federal courts of King County, Washington for any litigation or disputed arising out of or related to this Agreement, (b) you agree not to commence any litigation arising out of or related to this Agreement except in the state or federal courts mentioned herein, (c) you agree not to plead or claim that such litigation brought therein has been brought in an inconvenient forum. (d) EACH PARTY (you and the Publisher and any other unforeseen entity) HEREBY WAIVES ITS RIGHT TO A JURY TRIAL IN CONNECTION WITH ANY DISPUTE OR LEGAL PROCEEDING ARISING OUT OF THIS AGREEMENT OR THE SUBJECT MATTER HEREOF AND THEREOF.

LLLA 3: COMPLIANCE WITH EXPORT LAWS. You may not use or otherwise export or re-export any DBP product except as authorized by the Publisher and the United States law and the laws of the jurisdiction in which the DBP product was obtained. In particular, but without limitation, any DBP product may not be exported or re-exported (a) into any U.S. embargoed countries or (b) to anyone on the U.S. Treasury Department's list of Specially Designated Nationals or the U.S. Department of Commerce Denied Person's List or Entity List. By using any DBP product as licensed to you and specified in this EULA, you represent and warrant that you are not located in any such country or on any such list. You also agree that you will not use any DBP product for any purposes prohibited by United States of America law.

LLLA 4: The DBP product License Provided by Authorized Third Parties: The Publisher does not control, endorse, or accept responsibility for Any third party services. Any dealings between you and any authorized or unauthorized third party in connection with a Third Party Service or sell, including such party's privacy policies and use of your personal information, delivery of and payment for licenses fees and services, and any other terms, conditions, warranties, or representations associated with such dealings, are solely between you and such third party. Any DBP authorized third party agent must always abide by DBP's EULA and additional notarized agreements between authorized 3rd Party Agent and DBP. Any third party Authorized distributor of a DBP product license, as an agent for the Publisher, agrees to abide by its separate agreement with Publisher and also to abide by the Publisher's EULA outlined here. No third party is permitted to violate any Publisher sections in this agreement. Furthermore, any agent of the Publisher is to abide by all laws in the region in which it resides in so far as it does not violate this license agreement and the additional separate license agreement with Publisher. If you purchased a license of a DBP product via an authorized 3rd Party DBP agent and cannot find a suitable resolution to your issue, please bring it up directly to the Publisher at MiCostaBella@Gmail.Com. The Publisher will do its best to attempt to resolve your issue.

The Americans

If only for a Moment We Hold Hands
For The Arts!

Comprehending Only The Moment;

But Sustaining An Effort That Has
Prevailed!

D.Darseli Santana

5

The Americans 2nd Revised Edition
TABLE OF CONTENTS

CHAPTER ONE — The Introduction:
A Love of Acrobatics 9

CHAPTER TWO — Dario Lucas of Mexico City
Incredible Hand Balancer 11

CHAPTER THREE — The Childhood and Early Circus Life of
Luis Pimentel Ruiz   15

CHAPTER FOUR — Circo Arriola of Spain 19

CHAPTER FIVE — ¡El Cubano Pulsador! 33
Benito Hernández-Hand Balancer of Cuba

CHAPTER SIX — Colombia! ¡El País de Maravilla!   37

CHAPTER SEVEN — Happy Land Night Club 41
(Exploring Central America!)

CHAPTER EIGHT — Juarez-El Paso (The Beautiful Colors
of a U.S./Mexicn Border Region!) 51

CHAPTER NINE — Muscle Beach
(Santa Monica, California) 57

CHAPTER TEN — A Transition-Luis Pimentel Ruiz And
The Gang of Santa Monica Beach! 65

CHAPTER ELEVEN — Cisco The Kid -Arriba Arriba Arriba! 75

CHAPTER TWELVE — The Later Years- Luis Pimentel Ruiz
of Santa Monica California 86

CHAPTER THIRTEEN — The Passion Continues.....
CHRIS PIMENTEL OROZCO 91

CHAPTER FOURTEEN — Epilogue:
Acrobatic Definition-Performance
Evolution-Hand Balancing Techniques 92

THE
"AMERICANS"

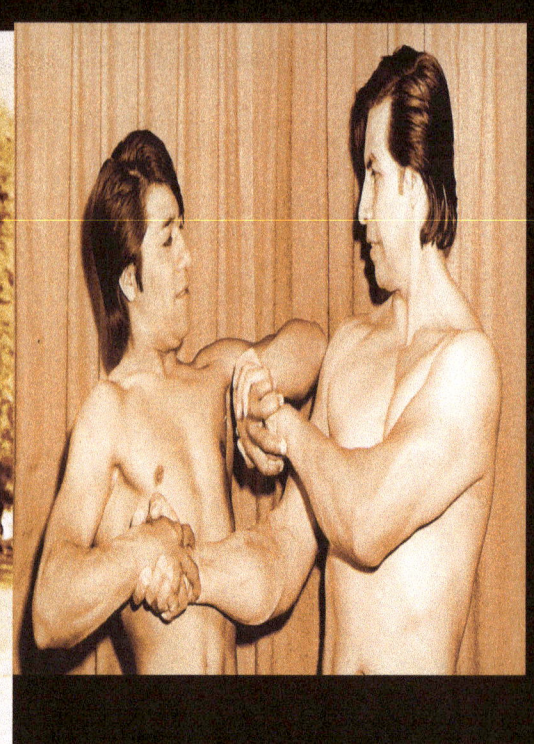

THE
"AMERICANS"

CHAPTER ONE
THE INTRODUCTION

There comes a time in everyone's life on this planet where youth abounds within us! The physical youth at our early age beckons us to physical activities that make the human body Happy! Excited! Challenged!

There are some that take this physical excitement and challenge to a continual level because it brings happiness and contentment. These individuals, who go against what the world expects, are the physical performers that make the physical activities one sees in the world as...

Fun! Exciting! Entertaining! Marvelous!

As an observer of these physical activities, one is inclined to say things like:

"How could they do that?"

"Wow!

"That definitely took a lot of dedication and
Will power to accomplish!"

One such physical performer that was drawn to the physical activities of high achievement was the Mexican performer: Luis Pimentel Ruiz

[Note: In Spanish speaking countries the father's name comes first, Pimentel, and then the mother's name: Ruiz; so his last name is the paternal "Pimentel"]

In this illustrative book, we explore the beauty that he chose to pursue.

A pursuit that continued because of the love he had for it.

It lasted a lifetime!

Some physical performers that take it to a continual level do physical activities like surfing, ball games, rock climbing, dancing!

Luis chose Hand Balancing a derivative of the Art of Acrobatics! ...although he was trained and mastered all forms of acrobatics.

In this art form there is a "base" and a "flyer". The "base" supports the "flyer" as he or she does feats in hand stand positions.

Since Luis Pimentel Ruiz's physical build was close to six feet tall, and with a strength that he built with continual perseverance, he usually took on the role of the "base" in the art form of hand-balancing. Yet, Luis served as a "flyer" on various occasions in his acrobatic career as well.

Although such physical endeavors did not bring him monetary riches, it brought him a personal achievement that cannot be easily replicated or experienced!

Here was a man that full-heartedly went after what he discovered:

Hand to Hand Balancing.

Luis Pimentel was on an adventure that started in his land of birth...

Michoacán, Mexico.

From there he ventured off to Mexico City, the rest of Mexico, and to Central and South America. In his travels he was performing feats of marvel that are documented in this book.

His adventure came to a close in Santa Monica, California...where the ocean breeze drew him in, with such intensity, that he decided to make this city his home of choice!

CHAPTER TWO
Luis Recruits The Experienced Hand Balancer
Dario Lucas
of
Mexico City

After moving to Santa Monica in 1963, at the age of 42, Luis Pimentel continued to have an interest in hand-to-hand balancing.

However, the economics of life obligated him to do his other profession of taper and painter in the construction industry...this paid the worldly bills!

Notwithstanding, after work, every day, rain or shine, Luis Pimentel Ruiz would spend a good amount of time at the beach with his family where they picnicked and practiced the art of hand balancing, and other acrobatics.

His family included: his wife, Margarita Pimentel Quiroga, his step-daughter María Rosario "Rosie" Martínez Quiroga (born 1950), his son Francisco "Cisco" Pimentel Quiroga (born 1956), and his daughter Janet Pimentel Quiroga (born 1961).

During this time, in his pursuit for a flyer, Luis created a hand-balancing act with his teenage step-daughter Rosie; a visual presentation of this duo will be seen later in this book. Additionally, Luis taught his preteen son "Cisco" how to do handstands, hand to hand balancing, somersaults and other acrobatic maneuvers. His son's enthusiasm grew to the point where Francisco became a competent and avid Acrobat.

Luis' wife, who had performed with him in a trio in South and Central America, was not actively performing anymore with Luis when they moved to Santa Monica. Notwithstanding, Margarita Pimentel Quiroga (maiden name: Margarita Quiroga Torres) continued to maintain an exercise regimen since that is what she had done since she was a child. Margarita comes from a family that owned a circus in Colombia, South America. Her family's involvement in circus performing dates back at least 150 years!

Although Rosie was doing a hand-to-hand balancing act with Luis for a while, it came to a definitive close in 1968. As Rosie took on other interests, Luis was left without a "flyer".

Yet hope for Luis to continue this art form that he loved was on the horizon!

During his time in Mexico, as a young lad, Luis had had a long connection with the acrobatic Lucas family of Mexico City.

This artistic family later furnished Luis, while in Santa Monica California, with an excellent hand balancing "flyer" by the name of...

Jose Dario Lucas
known simply as
"Dario"

Dario was the son of Santos Lucas.

Santos Lucas had worked with Luis back in Mexico City. Luis, in his early twenties, had a hand to hand balancing act decades before with Santos and his brother Filimón after having met while doing construction in the nation's capital. This will be documented later in this book.

Dario Lucas, with the help of Luis Pimentel, was brought to Santa Monica in 1970 to work with Luis on a hand to hand balancing act.

Dario was an experienced hand balancer who had worked at various circuses with his brother Jose Luis Lucas in Mexico before arriving to Santa Monica, California.

Luis had sent Dario a letter who received it while actively performing in a circus as a "flyer" in a hand balancing act. Dario's brother served as the "base" in a hand-balancing act with him. The letter came two weeks after they entered "Circo Unión" in Mexico.

Dario saw this as an opportunity and left the circus to join Luis in Santa Monica, California. His brother, Jose Luis, stayed in the circus; but now only under the capacity of a concession salesman!

So at the age of 50!.....Luis acquired a "flyer" to continue to pursue his profession in acrobatics!

Dario was 26 years younger than Luis!

This new duo performed regularly at carnivals and special events.

In an attempt to get more gigs, Luis had filmed a hand to hand balancing number with Dario and gave it to an agent who was supposed to get them more work performing. However, that never materialized. At the end, the 8 mm film was lost as this agent disappeared.

A short time later, the duo was approached by another agent that offered them work in Las Vegas and in Europe! But, Luis felt a loyalty to the other agent and declined. Thus, the opportunity to perform in Vegas and in Europe was erroneously given up because of loyalty issues!

This unsound decision left them with little work.

Consequently, after a while, Dario, pressured by his father, was forced to leave Luis in order to find work in another profession. Dario moved to Glendale, California and took on a full-time regular, blue-collar day job as a car washer at Glen-Rock Car Wash!

This shift in focus, little by little, drew Dario away from his acrobatic life he had known since the tender age of four.

Dario accepted this readily since he had to send money to his mother, brothers, and sisters back in Mexico City. For Dario, their livelihood was more important than to continue the precarious work that unfortunately, usually comes with an acrobatic occupation.

In a 2013 interview with the author of this book, Dario mentioned that he did not regret leaving the life of an acrobatic performer. He clearly stated that the unstable income was not good for any type of lifestyle. He had learned this fact in Mexico; but had hoped it would be different across the border. It was not.

Although Dario would visit Santa Monica on weekends and do some hand to hand balancing rehearsals with Luis, it was just that: rehearsals.

Luis wanted more, but without steady work, he could not convince Dario to continue with a physical activity that was so strongly and passionately embedded in Luis Pimentel Ruiz' mind and eyes.

13

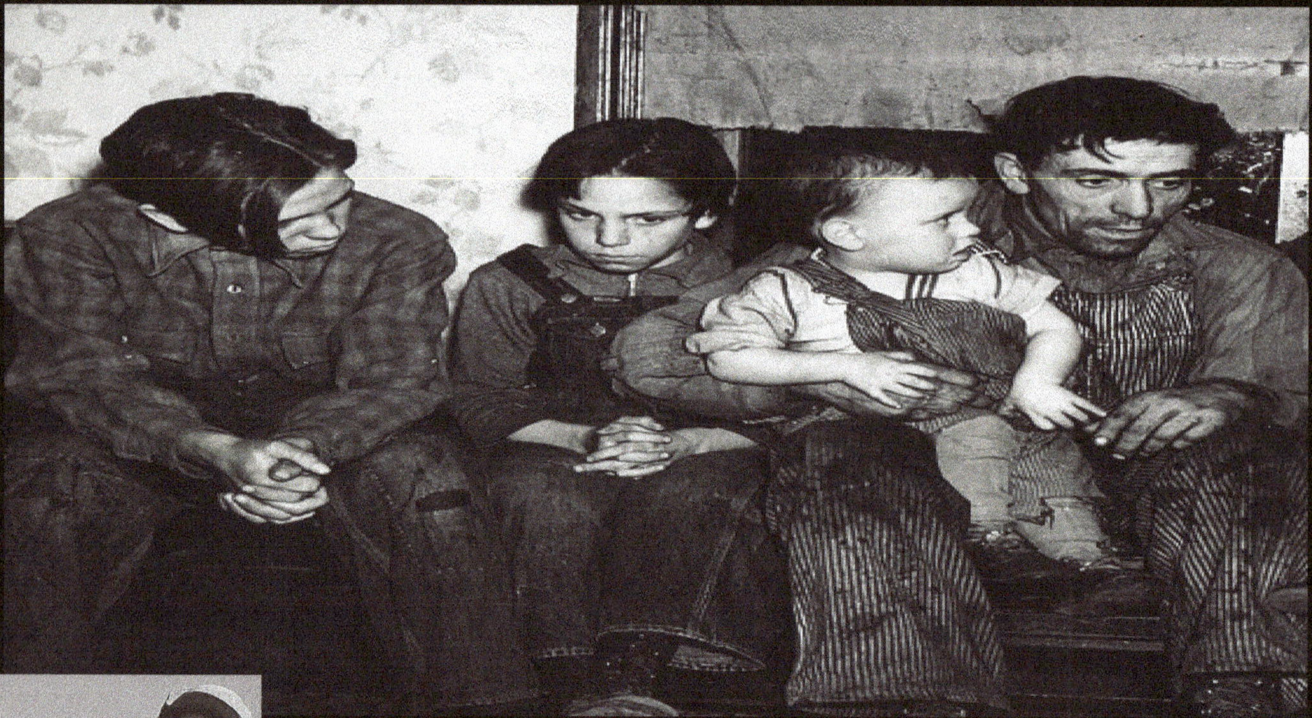

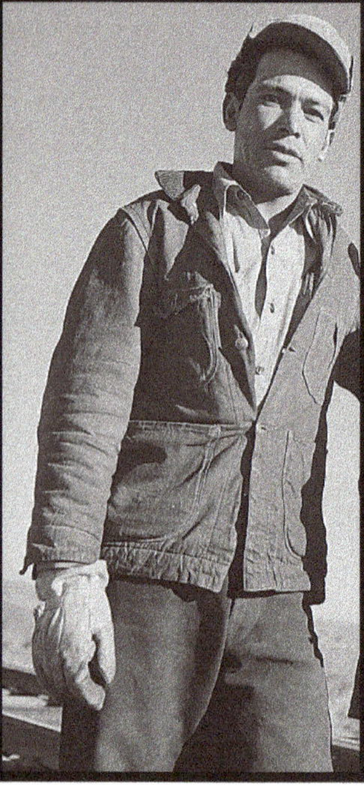

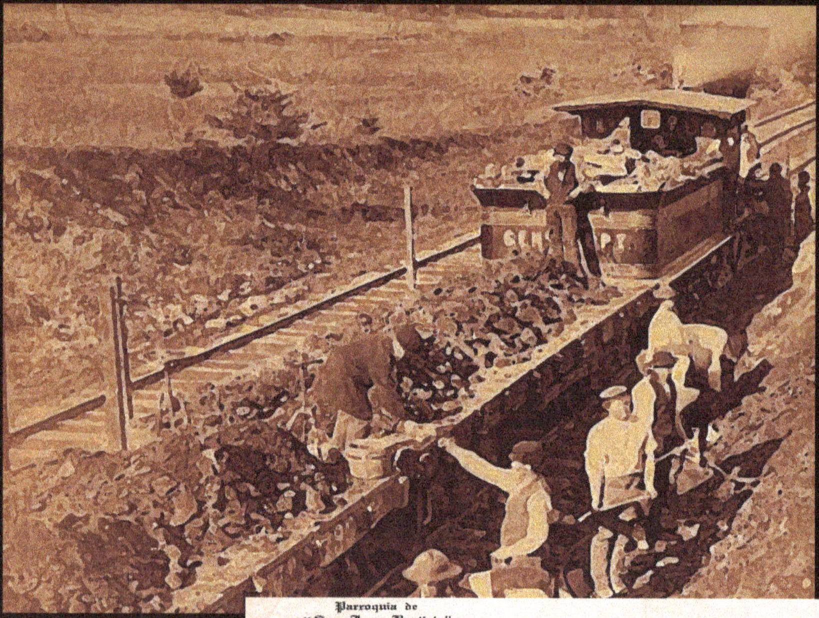

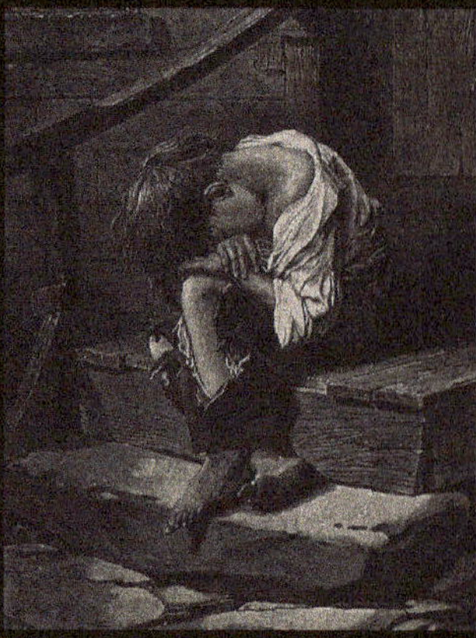

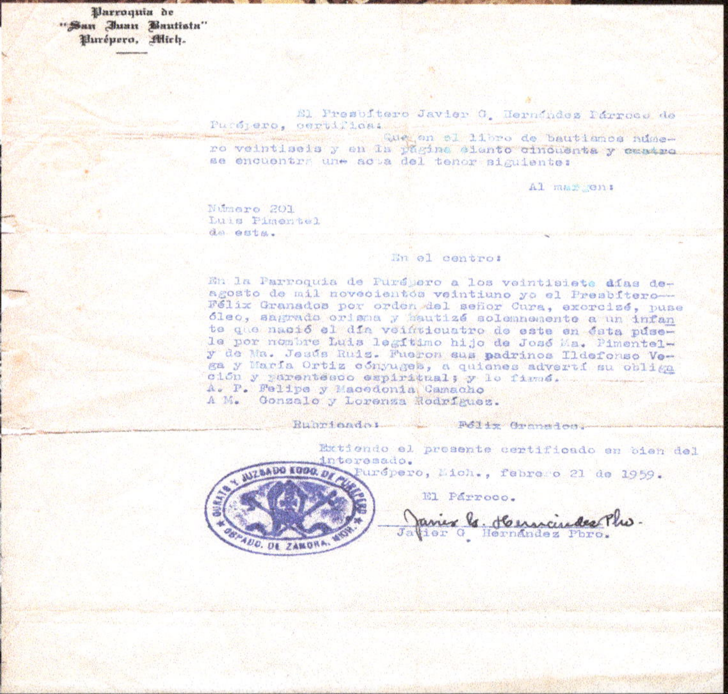

Parroquia de
"San Juan Bautista"
Purépero, Mich.

El Presbítero Javier G. Hernández Párroco de
Purépero, certifica:

Que en el libro de bautismos número
veintiséis y en la página ciento cincuenta y cuatro
se encuentra una acta del tenor siguiente:

Al margen:

Número 201
Luis Pimentel
de esta.

En el centro:

En la Parroquia de Purépero a los veintisiete días de
agosto de mil novecientos veintiuno yo el Presbítero——
Félix Granados por orden del señor Cura, exorcisé, puse
óleo, sagrado crisma y bauticé solemnemente a un infan-
te que nació el día veinticuatro de este en ésta pose-
le por nombre Luis legítimo hijo de José Ma. Pimentel-
y de Ma. Jesús Ruiz. Fueron sus padrinos Ildefonso Ve-
ga y María Ortiz cónyuges, a quienes advertí su obliga
ción y parentesco espiritual; y lo firmé.
A M. Felipe y Macedonia Camacho
A M. Gonzalo y Lorenza Rodríguez.

Rubricado: Félix Granados.

Extiendo el presente certificado en bien del
interesado.
Purépero, Mich., febrero 21 de 1959.

El Párroco.

Javier G. Hernández Pbro.

CHAPTER THREE
Luis' Childhood and Early Youth!

Luis Pimentel Ruiz was born at 9 at night on the 24 of August 1921...born in a House without a number!

...on a street named "Calle de Zaragoza"...which is in Purépero, Michoacán.
His father, José María Pimentel Camacho, was a day laborer who, like many poor Mexicans, looked for work where available. He apparently had no education. Little is known of his interests or past endeavors.

What is known though is that when Luis Pimentel Ruiz was about 5 years old in 1926, his father crossed the U.S.-Mexican border on his way to work on the U.S. SouthWest railroad construction endeavor paid for by the big railroad companies who were supported by the U.S. government: much of the track lands were given to them free of charge along with other perks: such as the easing of immigration laws for their neighbors to the South in order to obtain cheap labor.

Luis' mother, who bore three children in all, María Jesús Ruiz, died two years after Luis' birth of unknown causes. That left José María with three children to care for completely on his own. Luis was the youngest; the other two were about two and four years older...known to the author only as "el Zorro" and Fermín.

"el Zorro" had blue eyes. Luis had hazel green eyes. Luis' wife recalls though that his eyes changed from green to blue depending on the clothing he wore! El Zorro apparently was a muralist who did wall paintings. Fermín's occupation was unknown.

Luis' early childhood years were difficult: no mother and in poverty; despite the family of Luis belonging to an upscale family that worked for the government!

Luis' father left his three boys with "family" while he was forced to be a blue-collar laborer in the building of the railroads in the United States in order to sustain the livelihood for his children. José María gave this "family" a monthly stipend to care for and feed the children.

However, according to Luis Pimentel, in conversations he had with the author of this book, things were not good. He was always hungry and had to resort to look for food in the town's garbage cans. Apparently, Luis Pimentel the child was not fed adequately by those who were entrusted to care for the three when José María left to help build the railroads.

Because of this type of childhood, Luis HATED Mexico.

Luis, unfortunately, experienced severe poverty throughout his childhood.

However, luck found its way!

Circa 1933, the Mexican President (Lázaro Cárdenas y del Río) happened to be walking the streets of Michoacán on a political campaign. Young Luis heard the crowd. Luis immediately ran up to Cárdenas and pleaded for help. The President's bodyguards were about to remove young Luis. However, Lázaro told them to wait.

Lázaro felt compassion for young Luis, who was about 12 years old.

Luis explained his situation and told the President that he wanted to learn!

With that request, Lázaro ordered his secretaries who were with him to give young Luis entrance into the preparatory school reserved for families of military officials.

15

Lázaro was a revolutionary General before he became Governor of Michoacán (1928 to 1932) and President of Mexico (1934-1940), and thus was well connected with the schools.

Luis attended one of these privileged schools till circa his 18th birthday, and was scheduled to continue his education. However, Lázaro's Presidency was coming to a close and Luis found himself without a benefactor.

Mexican President Lázaro Cárdenas y del Río during his Military Career. This is the Man that Helped Luis as he campaigned the streets of Michoacan.
Original Photograph taken by a Polish Photographer.

Gobierno del Estado de Michoacán de Ocampo
Archivo del Poder Ejecutivo

CERTIFICADO NUMERO 51,145 EL CIUDADANO LICENCIADO – EMILIO SOLORZANO SOLIS, JEFE DEL DEPARTAMENTO DEL ARCHIVO DEL PODER EJECUTIVO DEL ESTADO DE MICHOACAN DE OCAMPO.– – – – –

CERTIFICA:– Que en el libro duplicado de actas de –– NACIMIENTO, levantadas en el Juzgado del Registro Civil de –– PUREPERO, MICHOACAN, durante el año de 1921 y a fojas sin nú-mero del tomo I, se encuentra asentada la que sigue:– Al mar-gen.– Acta número 142.– Nacimiento de LUIS PIMENTEL.– Al cen-tro.– En la Villa de Purépero del Estado de Michoacán de Ocam po, a las 6 seis de la tarde del día 2 dos del mes de Septiem bre del año de 1921 mil novecientos veintiuno, ante el infras crito Juez, y en esta Oficina el Señor José María Pimentel –– presentó un niño vivo nacido a las 9 nueve de la noche del –– día 24 veinticuatro de Agosto último en una casa sin número – de la Calle de Zaragoza a quien se puso por nombre y apellido LUIS PIMENTEL, hijo no legítimo del compareciente a quien re-conoce por suyo en toda forma lo que se hace constar a su pe-tición.– Se levanta la presente ante los Ciudadanos Rubén Pi-mentel y José Sepúlveda mayores de edad, vecinos de este lu-gar y sin parentesco con los interesados; quienes leída que – les fué esta acta, se manifestaron conformes y firman los que saben hacerlo.– Doy fé.– Firmados.– Ezequiel B. Cerda.– Rubén Pimentel.– S. Sepúlveda.– Es copia fiel de su original que – certifico.– Una firma ilegible.– – – – – – – – – – – – – – – ––

SE EXPIDE LA PRESENTE, en la Ciudad de Morelia, ––– Michoacán, a los 18 días del mes de Agosto de 1986 mil nove–– cientos ochenta y seis.– – – – – – – – – – – – – – – – – –

DOCUMENTACION Y REGISTRO

1ma

Recibo Número 2211436-C

Importe $375.00

MICHOACAN DE OCAMPO
GOBIERNO DEL ESTADO
ARCHIVO DEL PODER EJECUTIVO

Oficialía Mayor – Dirección de Documentación y Registro

To the Right Next Page: Luis Pimentel Ruiz doing a Hand Stand in Front of the Circus Tent of the Circus He joined! Indeed, he learned much acrobatics as a Circus Apprentice and Circus Helper.

Luis pondered what to do next...either find a way to somehow continue his education or start another endeavor.

During this contemplative time, on a fateful day, a circus was in town and Luis decided to visit it.

In this Mexican circus, Luis saw a very strong man (a body builder). Young 18 year old Luis decided that he wanted to be just like him: STRONG! So Luis joined the circus as a circus helper. He cleaned up after the animals and helped buildup and teardown the circus canopy at every city and town in Mexico the circus went to do business.

Luis became FASCINATED!!!

And from that moment on, Luis decided that that is what he wanted to do.

In retrospect, Luis recalled to his son Francisco that one day he had fallen asleep and that the circus left without him. Young Luis awoke distraught and asked were the circus had gone. Luis followed the train tracks by foot for a day and a half and ultimately reunited with the circus!

In another incident during this initiation to circus life, a truck on an incline was moving backwards and heading toward a woman. Luis raced toward the truck and was able to halt it with his body's strength two feet from the woman!

His physical strength had AUGMENTED!

Circus life was fascinating to Luis. He began to feel very comfortable as to the direction he had decided to take after he attended the privileged preparatory school.

CHAPTER FOUR
Mexico City - The Lucas Years

After about three years of travel, work, and training in the circus, Luis decided to take time off. Luis took on a day laborer job in Mexico City. His job was to assist in the tearing down of old buildings: participating in bulldozing them with a hammer in hand!

The job paid a decent wage; allowing him to rent a small place to stay and to purchase food to eat.

Two of his coworkers, Santos Lucas and Filimón Lucas, brothers, had a pass to a gymnasium, compliments of their foreman. They invited Luis to join them and they began to regularly go in and use the facility to help build and maintain their strength.

It turned out that the brothers had also been in a circus and were (out of all things possible) hand balancers!

Luis was very enthusiastic about a possible partnership with them. He urged the brothers to train with him at a local park after work in order to make a trio performance act at a circus. They agreed.

After several weeks of practicing, they had created an act that they felt was ready for a circus performance. So off they went in search of a circus that would contract them for their performance. They called themselves "Los Tres Enmascarados"...the Three Masked Men.

Their first attempt was at a small circus. After the owner had seen the act, he was amazed and told them that he would not be able to pay for such a strong performance. However, the small circus owner did refer them to a bigger circus called "Circo Arriola". This bigger circus was a travelling circus from Spain in the Americas!

The trio was contracted immediately when the owners saw their act. Luis, having been trained in his first circus to be both "base" and "flyer", became the base for the trio since he was the tallest and strongest of the three. In Spanish, hand-balancing performers are called "Pulsadores".

Luis loved to be a performer!... and, as mentioned before, he enjoyed the art form of a "Pulsador" SO MUCH that it became a lifelong endeavor. The partnership with the brothers was good.

Since their act had many marvelous acrobatic feats, they constantly trained and rehearsed their number daily to avoid injury. They needed to keep their bodies in check. So when they did the number in front of an audience, it was a piece of cake. The hard work of being conditioned and ready was done daily during rehearsals.

Previous page: The Trio at the park where they rehearsed regularly in Mexico City. The Tower formation, which was photographed before its completion, was taken on top of a huge rock in a beach in Mexico.

19

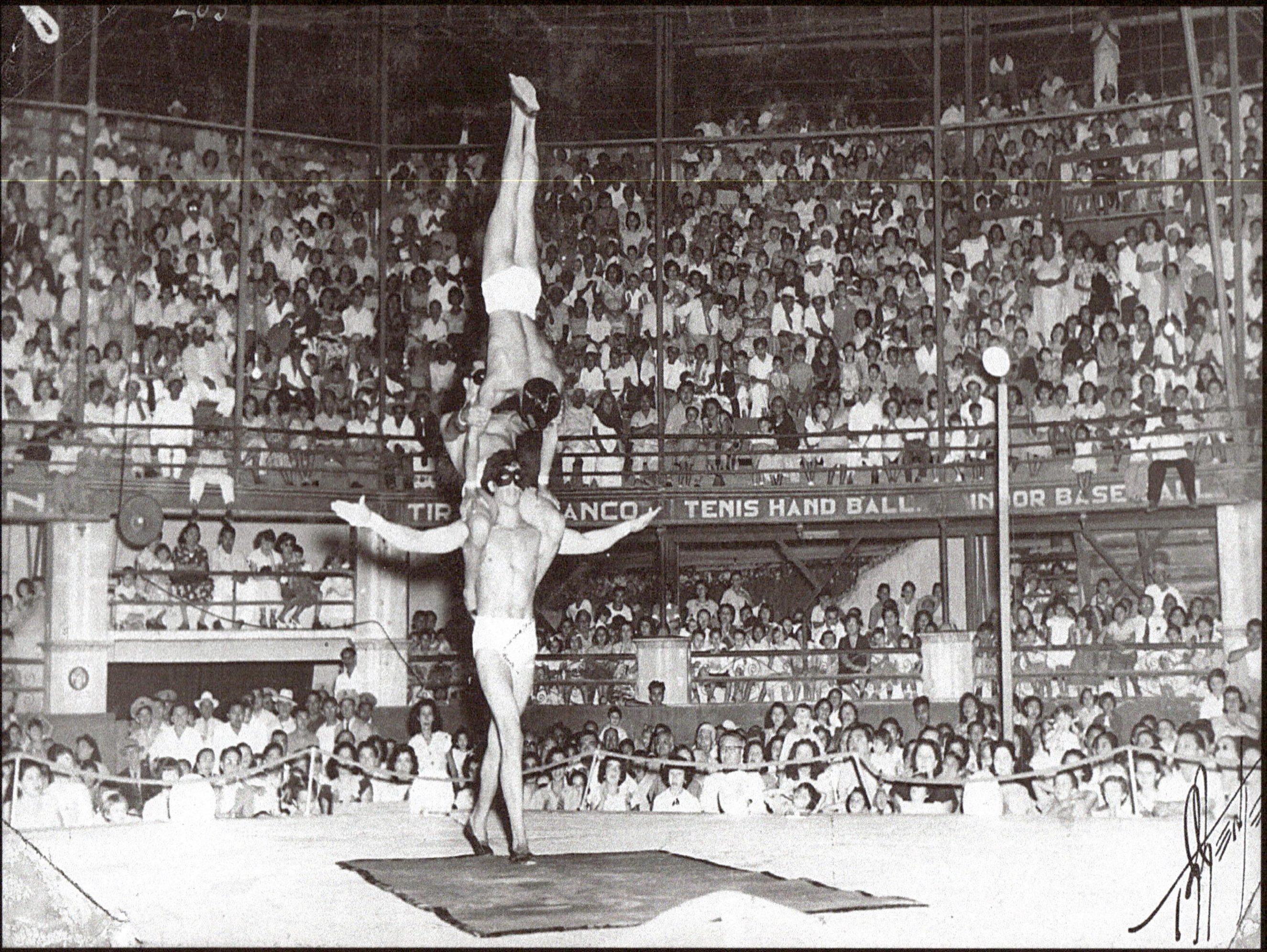
TENIS HAND BALL.

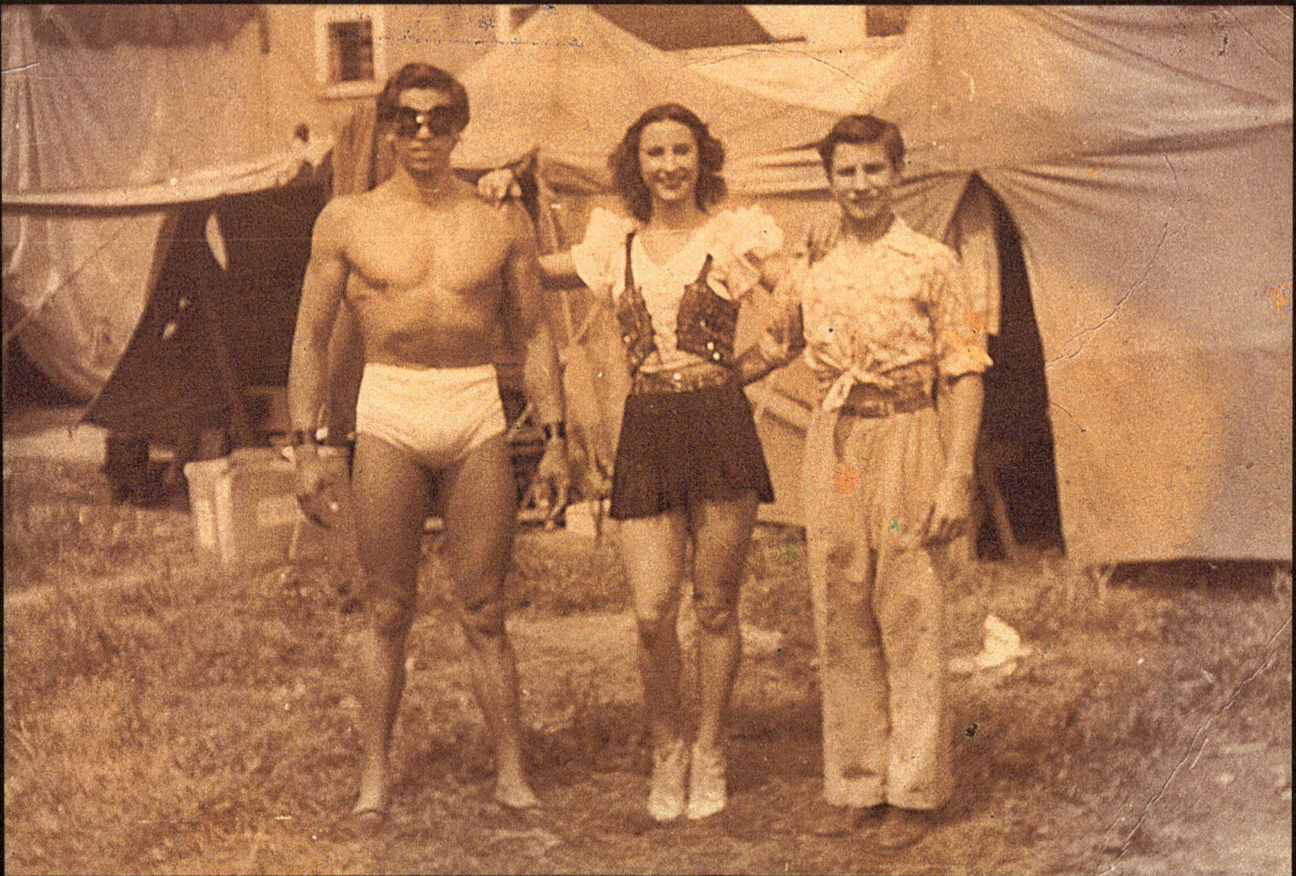

It is important to note that these athletes ate a lot of food daily! The exertions demanded by their acrobatic art form required a large amount of energy. The calories they gained through food were quickly used up in their daily intensive physical activities!

In Circo Arriola, Luis fell in love with one of the Arriola's:

Coral Arriola.

He loved her outgoing personality, and had a great admiration for her kindness.

However, Luis was shy and never mustered up the courage to confess his feelings for her. He kept them inside. In a conversation with Luis Pimentel Ruiz more than 5 decades later, the author of this book was told by Luis Pimentel Ruiz that he regretted not telling her how he felt about her. It was obvious in Luis' face and words during this interview that he truly loved this woman.

So all readers out there... muster up the courage!

21

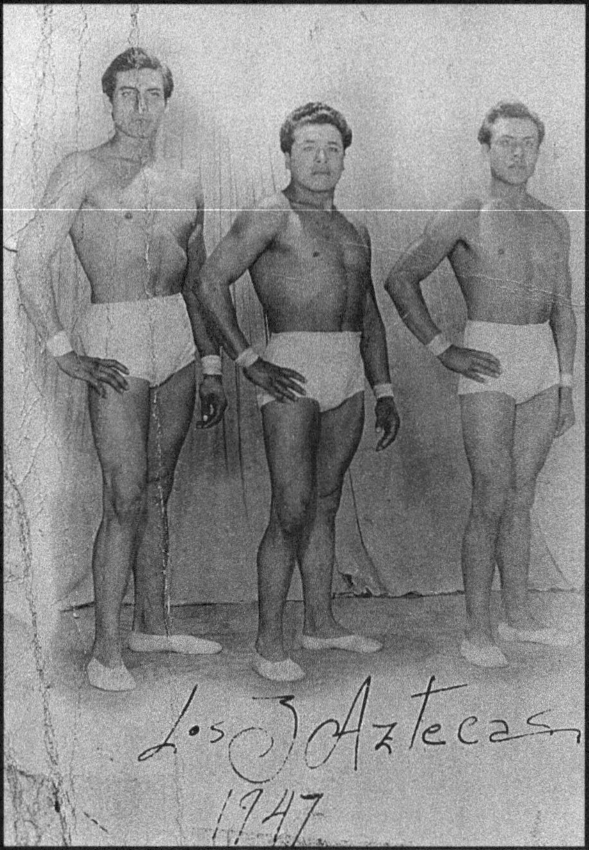

Los 3 Aztecas
1947

Filimón Lucas
Luis Pimentel
Santos Lucas
Guadalajara
"Pulseadores"
Jalisco

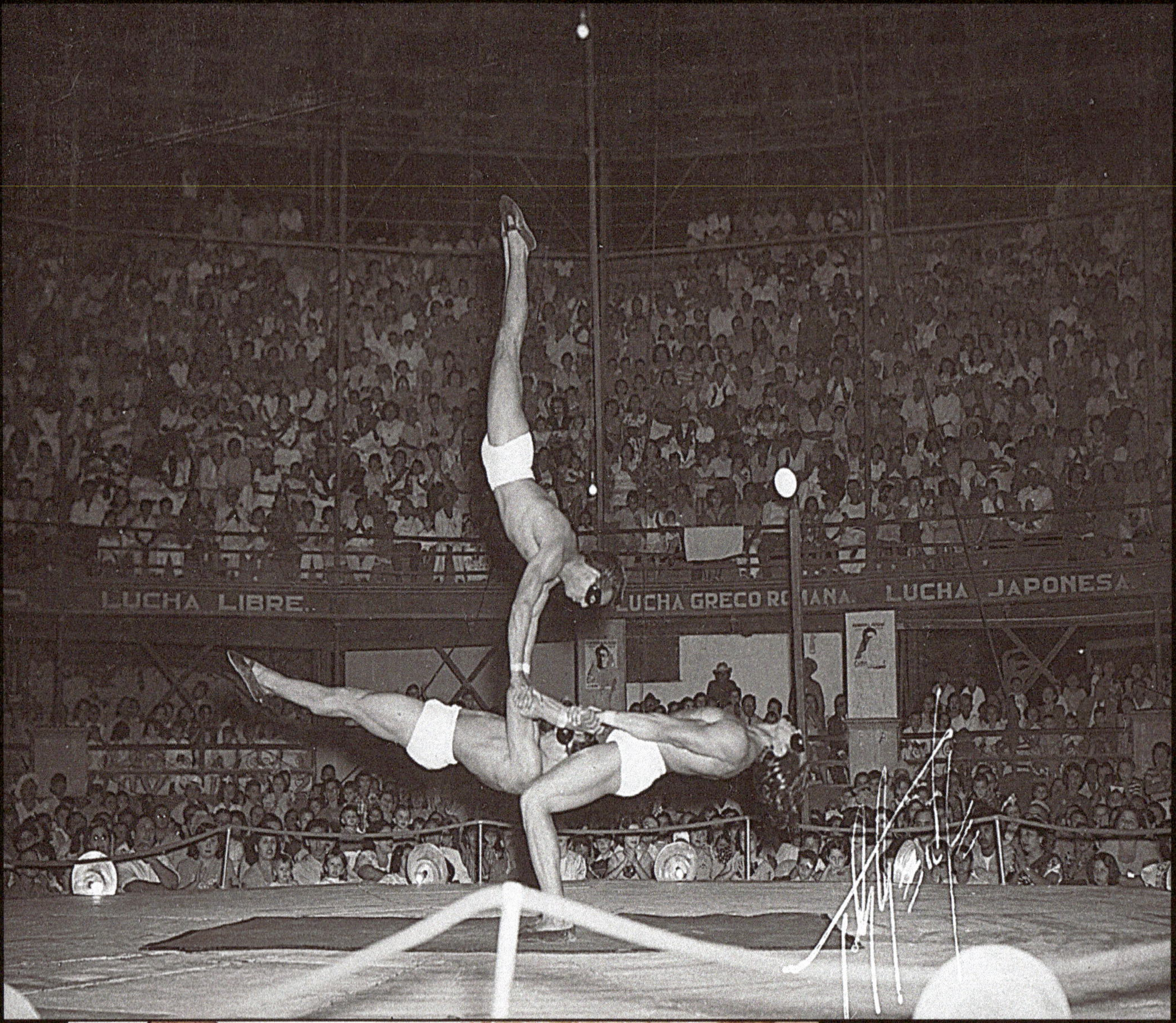
LUCHA LIBRE..
LUCHA GRECO ROMANA.
LUCHA JAPONESA.

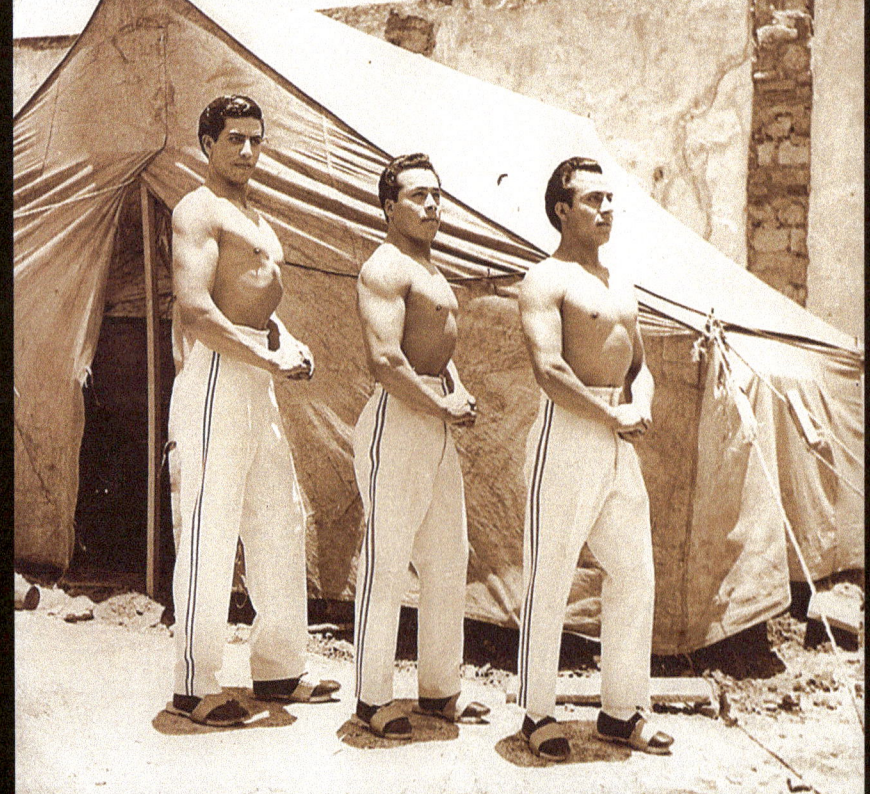

Los Caballeros Aguila

Los Tres Enmascarados

Around 1950, Luis, at the age of 30, had grown very STRONG and carried a GREAT PHYSIQUE! This led him to be spotted by Mexican movie producers who encouraged him to take photos in order to try out for a possible "Mexican" Tarzan type movie. Luis went ahead and took the pictures of himself as a jungle man figure. He was offered work as an actor.

During this time he met Ricardo Montalbán, a young actor then, who did handstands in his spare time. He actually did a short hand balancing routine with Luis on the spot! During this time Luis also met John Wayne, who was visiting Mexico on a production.

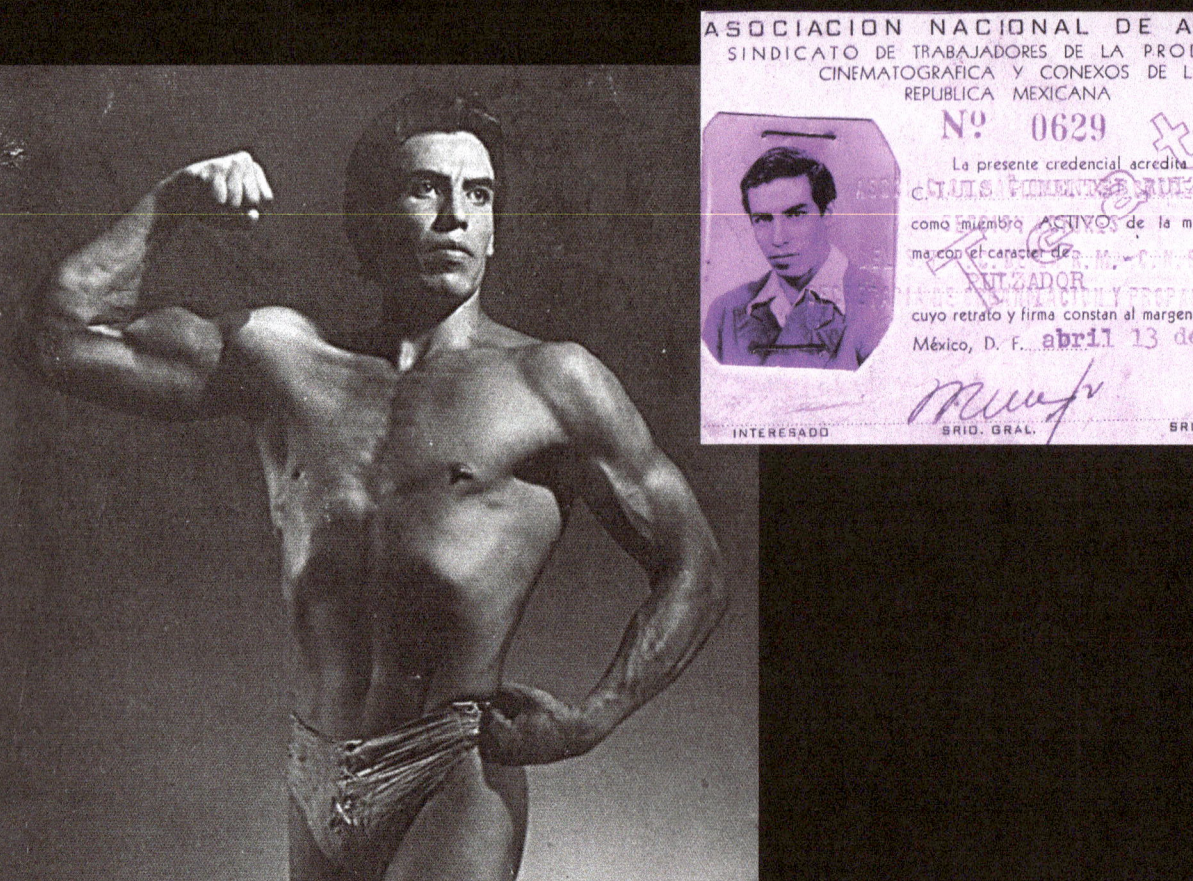

ASOCIACION NACIONAL DE ACTORES
SINDICATO DE TRABAJADORES DE LA PRODUCCION CINEMATOGRAFICA Y CONEXOS DE LA REPUBLICA MEXICANA

Nº 0629

La presente credencial acredita al C. [illegible]
como miembro ACTIVO de la misma con el caracter de [illegible]
PULZADOR
cuyo retrato y firma constan al margen
México, D. F. abril 13 de 195[illegible]

SECCION ACTORES

IGUALDAD DERECHO JUSTICIA

C.N.E.

INTERESADO SRIO. GRAL. SRIO. TESORERO

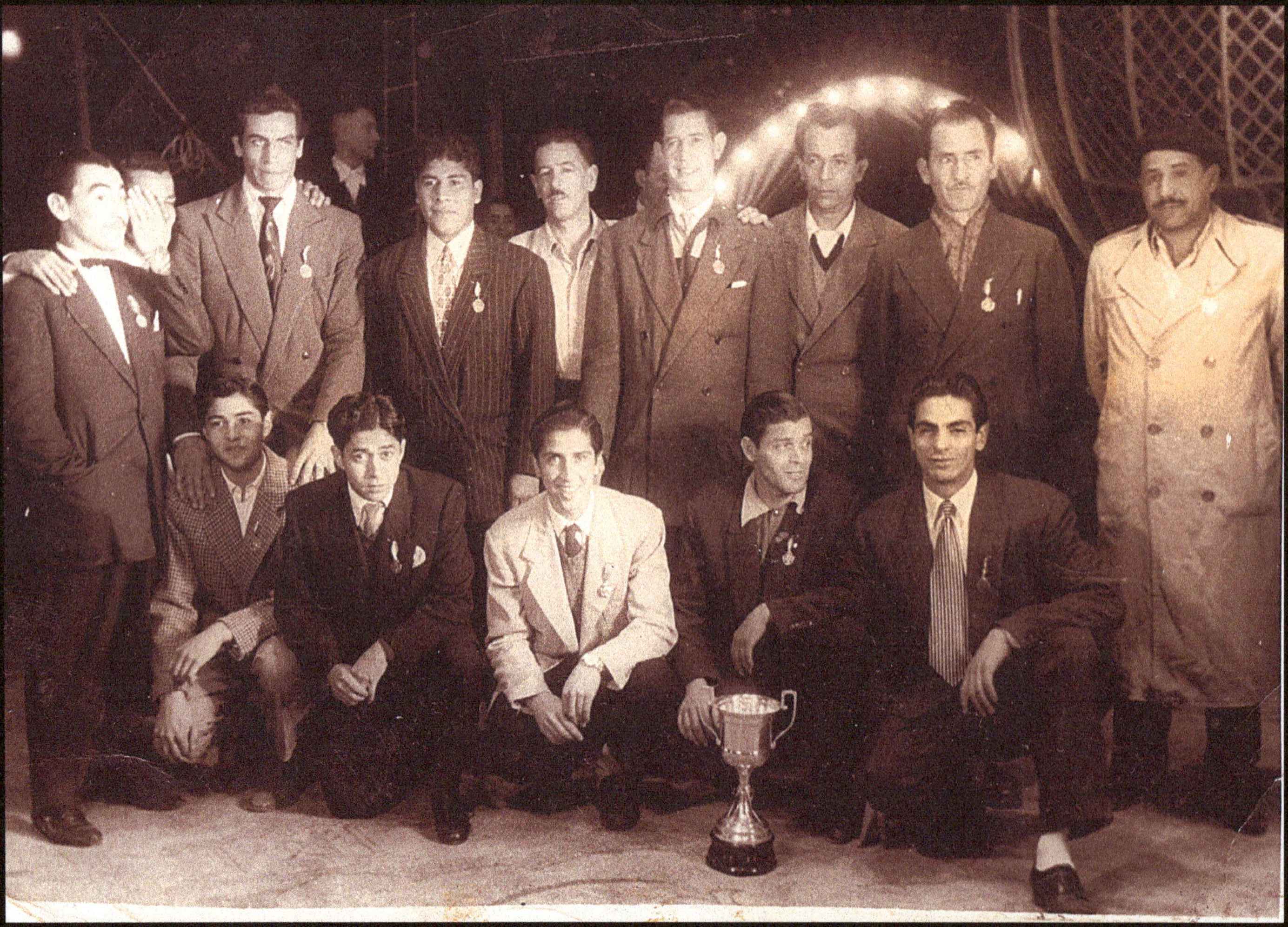

The pressure was on Luis to decide to continue with the trio or to continue as an actor!

At the end Luis' love for the art of hand balancing led him to decline the ongoing acting offer and continue with the trio. That is, Luis CHOSE UNCERTAINTY of money over a guaranteed contract that promised him a good CHUNK of change!

In 1950, the contract was up with Circo Arriola and the trio was offered work in Guatemala (Central America) with another circus. The trio headed to Guatemala.

However, the partnership with the brothers came to a close when there was a serious mishap amongst them, and Luis felt betrayed. In their rehearsals, it seemed that one of the brothers intentionally sought to injure Luis as he performed. It happened TWICE!... and seemed to be intentional. Luis decided he had had enough; he parted ways from the Lucas brothers in Guatemala.

DIRECTORES:
  MIGUEL ARRIOLA
        Y
  JOSE ARRIOLA

ADMINISTRACION:
  A. DE ARRIOLA

CONTABLE:
  E. ARRIOLA

SOCIEDAD:
  HNOS. ARRIOLA

DIRECCION FIJA:
  "VILLA ARRIOLA" CAMAS
  (SEVILLA) ESPAÑA. TEL. 250

GRANDES CIRCOS
ARRIOLA
ARRIOLA

Merida Yuc. II/4/50

"Los Tres Enmascarados" Trabajron en el circo Español Arriola durante una larga temporado Yo el empresario del circo D. José Arriola quedando muy satisfecho por la conducta y puntualidad en el trabajo de estos muchachos, lo hago constar en esta carta, para que sirva de base a cualquier otra empresa que quiera contratarlos, y para darle valor a estas letras lo hago contar con mi firma, en Merida Yuc. alos once del mes de abril de mil novecientos cincuenta

José Arriola   E. Arriola   Adela de Arriola

31

Benito Hernández and Luis Pimentel Ruiz

Luis Pimentel Ruiz doing a Handstand on the Humerus part of the arms of Benito

CHAPTER FIVE
Benito Hernández
¡El Cubano Pulsador!

Up to this point in time of departure, Luis had been performing for 12 years in various circuses in Mexico and Guatemala. And immediately after the departure from the Lucas brothers, As luck would have it, Luis Pimentel found a "flyer" within the circus he had been contracted in with the Lucas brothers. The flyer (**pulsador**) was a Cuban by the name of Benito Hernandez.

Luis expressed to the author that Benito was an INCREDIBLE pulsador.

In a conversation with the author of this book, Luis mentioned that out of all the people he had performed hand balancing acts with: Benito was CLEARLY the MOST REFINED in his skill as a flyer. Luis had never done, before or after, a hand balancing number with such a **well-trained athlete**!

Decades later, Luis' wife recalls that Benito would easily do a handstand on her shoulders. She was amazed that she did not feel any discomfort! It was an EXTREMELY SMOOTH execution of a handstand on a human body!

Since their act was extraordinary, Luis and Benito, after their short stint with a Guatemalan circus endeavor, were able to get a contract with a magician named "Mago Chang" in late 1950.

The Magician show of Mago Chang first featured the magician's act. As a final act of the show, the Atenienses (the Athenians), as the duo of Benito and Luis were called, would appear as statues, painted white.

The audience became shocked when the physically fit statues started to move!

Their amazement increased as they saw these statues begin to do an incredible hand-to-hand balancing act; something extraordinary they had never seen before.

The partnership with the magician took them to all the countries of Central America, especially to a prestigious theater in the Costa Rican Capital of San Jose called Teatro Nacional de Costa Rica (The National Theater of Costa Rica). From there they traveled to Colombia where the partnership with the magician "Mago Chang" ended in 1951.

Immediately after their departure from the magician in Colombia, South America, they were immediately hired by a large Colombian circus named **Circo Royal Dumbar**, which toured all over South America.

The Royal Dumbar circus in those days was considered "BIG". It had very good performers whose acts were unique. The circus was conducted under a "BIG TOP" tent. The owner was an "elegant and handsome" man by the name of **Alfonso Velasco**.

Benito, by that time, had already hooked up with his woman, a Colombian named Gloria. She became part of their number in order to highlight their presentation as they began their contract with the circus.

It was in Royal Dumbar that Luis found his future wife: Margarita Quiroga Torres: a Columbian woman who came from a long line of circus performers that spanned over 150 years!

Margarita was a single mother at that time **with a two year-old female child named "Rosie".** Back in those times in Colombia, it was not seen well to have a child out of wedlock. Accordingly, three of her five brothers did not allow her to return home since she had become pregnant.

This cultural action of rejection by her older brothers due to her pregnancy and later the birth of her child lead her to Royal Dumbar circus with her 2 and a half

Above: Margarita enjoying a Colombian water fall.

Above: Performing in Baranquilla. Below: three clown performers, and Margarita's cousin (left) and sister Olga (right) (both of which are visiting Margarita).

Above: Margarita's Sister, Olga Maria, holding Clown's Right Arm. She was visiting Margarita during this photo in a Dumbar tent .

year old daughter, Maria Rosario "Rosie" Martinez Quiroga (**who later became the mother of the author of this book you are reading!**).

Margarita had a very difficult pregnancy being homeless and finding shelter in an abandoned hut with dirt floors. Some female prostitutes helped her during this time, but would not allow her to go to where they worked. They protected her innocence! Margarita had gotten pregnant by force of a man who was her boyfriend. She was unable to veer him off her.

It is important to point out that Margarita's father was Adán Quiroga and that somehow the government by accident reversed the order of **her name**; where it should have been properly documented as Margarita Quiroga Torres...having the father's name go before the mother's: **Agueda Torres**.

Luis, Benito, Gloria, and Margarita traveled to various places with the Royal Dumbar circus. Once they went to Ecuador and had left young Rosie behind with a babysitter for the leg to Ecuador. This was heartbreaking for Margarita as is illustrated in the photos in Ecuador. Also, she kept her distance from Luis because she did not want to seem she was with him since at that point they had not married, but were dating.

After their circus endeavor in Colombia, Luis and his three performing companions continued with their hand-to-hand balancing act in Colombia. They appeared in night clubs and cultural events such as bull fights!

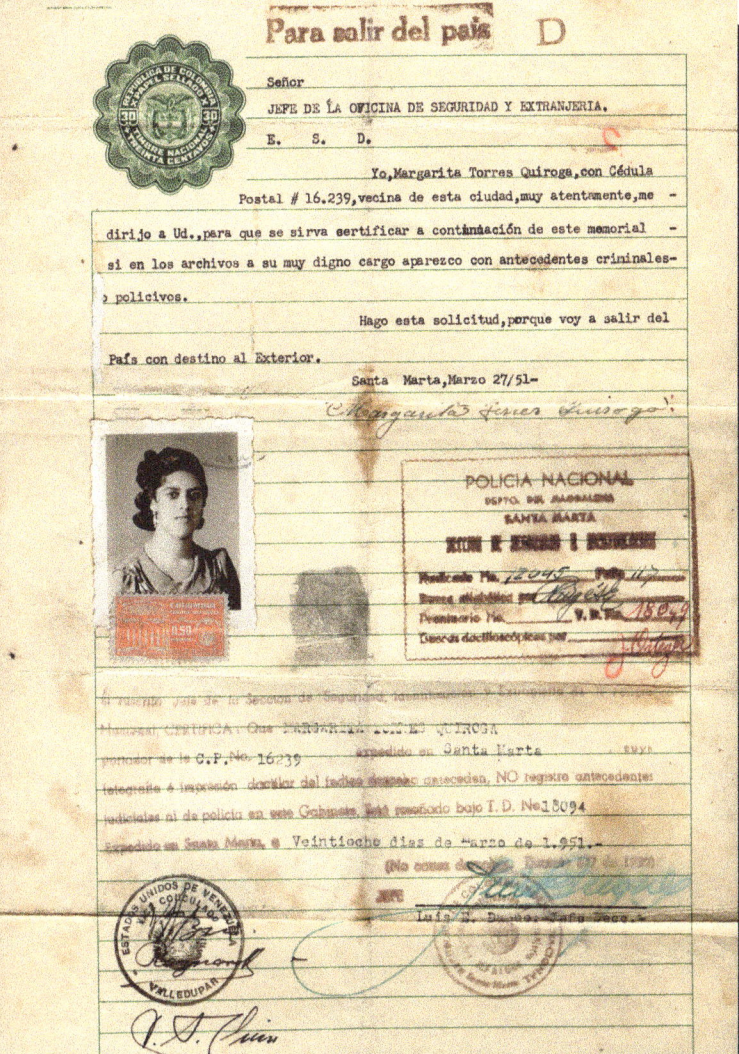

Above: Margarita With a cousin and her three year old daughter Rosie in 1953. Photogaph was taken at a beach in Barranquilla, Colombia.

35

To the Left: Circo Royal Dumbar Off to Ecuador. Luis Pimentel Ruiz far left;

Margarita Center with a Sad Face: she had to leave Little Rosie with a baby sitter. Benito, and Wife Gloria holding her poodle...far right.

Below Right, Luis in Ecuador with his adopted Dumbar family.

Below Left: Luis and Benito Performing On Stage in Ecuador with live Orchestra.

CHAPTER SIX
¡Mi Querida Colombia!
¡El País de Maravilla!

Luis Pimentel Ruiz was in a foreign land in Colombia! But he felt welcomed. The people around him were extremely friendly.

A Mexican Athlete in Colombia!

Luis enjoyed performing with Benito. As always, they kept their training consistent, on a daily basis, so that when the performance came, it was just like any other rehearsal; with the exception that they had an audience that appreciated the dedication these two men had for the art form of hand-to-hand balancing.

In addition to this physical activity, Luis Pimentel Ruiz entered the world of
"¡Lucha Libre!"
...free style wrestling. He entered it in order to earn extra money. Luis had learned wrestling back in Mexico with the STRONG MAN he met as a teenager.

The job of a wrestler was demanding. Accordingly, Luis did all he could in order to keep himself from injury, since he had the hand-to-hand balancing act going on at the SAME TIME!

During the matches, the situation sometimes got out of hand because of hot tempers amongst the wrestlers. But overall, Luis accomplished his goal of not getting injured to the point where he might have had to take time off.

When the author of this book was a child, he would look at his grandfather Luis Pimentel Ruiz and wonder why his ears were so small and shriveled up. Now it is understood that it came with the constant wrestling matches he had from Mexico to Central America to Colombia!

Back then, using head gear was not heard of; and so there were some permanent consequences that came with the sport!

Nonetheless, Luis loved the matches, but not as much as the art form of hand balancing.

Left: Luis Pimentel Ruiz Wrestling in Colombia.

37

Los Famosos "Pulsadores," Los Atenienses, Están en esta Ciudad

Han recorrido todo el continente - Esperan presentarse en la capital vallecaucana muy pronto.

La figura de Luis Pimentel Ruiz, excelente artista mexicano, es suficientemente conocida por la afición local. Hombre de grandes actitudes, en donde quiera que le ha ya correspondido actuar ha sobresalido ampliamente. Cuando vino el famoso mago 'Chang' a Cali, en el año de 1951, Pimentel Ruiz vino haciendo parte de la 'trouppe' artística actuando como 'pulseador', al lado de otros magníficos elementos, formando el grupo denominado 'Atenienses' que, para decir lo cierto, conquistó merecidos triunfos en nuestro medio. Era aquel un grupo único en su género; la fuerza, el ritmo y la precisión, llegaron a tener categoría de arte, con lo cual no pudieron menos que recibir los aplausos del público aficionado.

'Los Atenienses', con sus recursos magníficos, han recorrido el hemisferio Occidental, empezando por México, para pasar luego a todos los países Centroamericanos, más tarde al Perú, Ecuador y Colombia. Su prestigio cundió por todas partes, pues Luis Pimentel y su admirable grupo supieron convencer al público.

En Cali

El público deportista de la capital vallecaucana tuvo la oportunidad de admirar el gran valor y recursos incomparables del luchador Febo de Atenas, nombre con el cual Ruiz Pimentel saltó a los cuadriláteros, con ocasión de la pasada temporada internacional de lucha libre, conquistando, como era de esperarse, triunfos que la crítica contabilizó a su favor en merecidos elogios.

Previous page-suited men Image: Luis being recognized for his artistic achievement by a local Colombian mayor.

In the previous page article, Luis was recognized by a local offical in Cali, Colombia for his athletic excellence; demonstrating clearly his abilities as a Pulsador and Luchador! This article about him was featured in a local newpaper.

Previous page: During training, Luis Wrestles Greco-Roman style with Another Foreigner in Colombia; a Wrestler from the United States of America

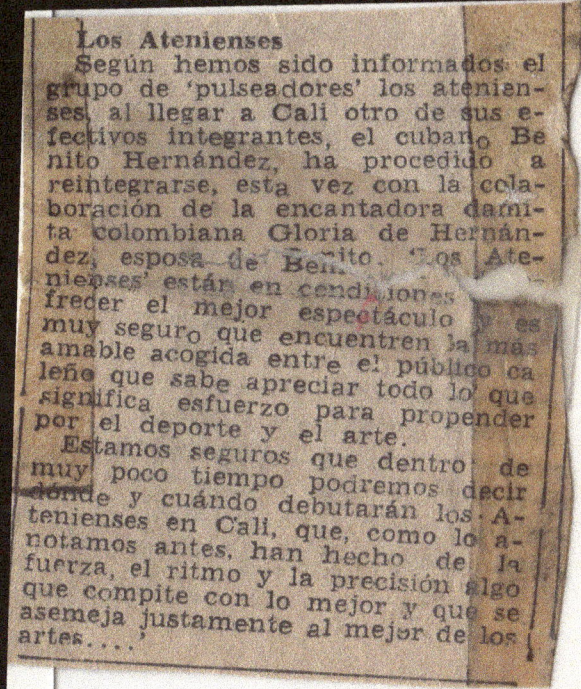

Los Atenienses
Según hemos sido informados el grupo de 'pulseadores' los atenienses, al llegar a Cali otro de sus efectivos integrantes, el cubano Benito Hernández, ha procedido a reintegrarse, esta vez con la colaboración de la encantadora damita colombiana Gloria de Hernández, esposa de Benito. Los Atenienses están en condiciones freder el mejor espectáculo es muy seguro que encuentren la más amable acogida entre el público caleño que sabe apreciar todo lo que significa esfuerzo para propender por el deporte y el arte.
Estamos seguros que dentro de muy poco tiempo podremos decir donde y cuándo debutarán los Atenienses en Cali, que, como lo anotamos antes, han hecho de la fuerza, el ritmo y la precisión algo que compite con lo mejor y que se asemeja justamente al mejor de los artes....

Luis photographed with children of Circo Royal Dumbar, Colombia... known as "Niños De Oro". As can be scene, it was common to live in tents as one traveled from one town to the next. Life was not always easy traveling in this manner, but the friendships made up for it.

After about 3 years in Colombia and other countries in South America, Luis decided to head back to Central America in route to Mexico. Their last performances were in Barranquilla, Colombia; a beach resort city near Panama.

Their next stop was Colon, Panama.

So in 1954, they traveled to Panama by boat. The boat was filled with foreign performing artists of all sorts on top, and animals at the bottom. Margarita had obtained permission to leave the country with her daughter and headed, for the first time, out of South America!

Margarita was sad because that meant an unknown farewell to her parents whom she loved dearly, along with her brothers and sisters.

Margarita felt that it was worth to take the risk and to leave a culture that caused one of her older brothers to reject her and banish her from her parent's home in Girardot. And even though this older brother apologized and promised to take care of her and her child, she did not want to take a risk of this brother rebelling again against her for something she had no control over.

A Boat similar to this one took the trio and other artists to Colon, Panama.

39

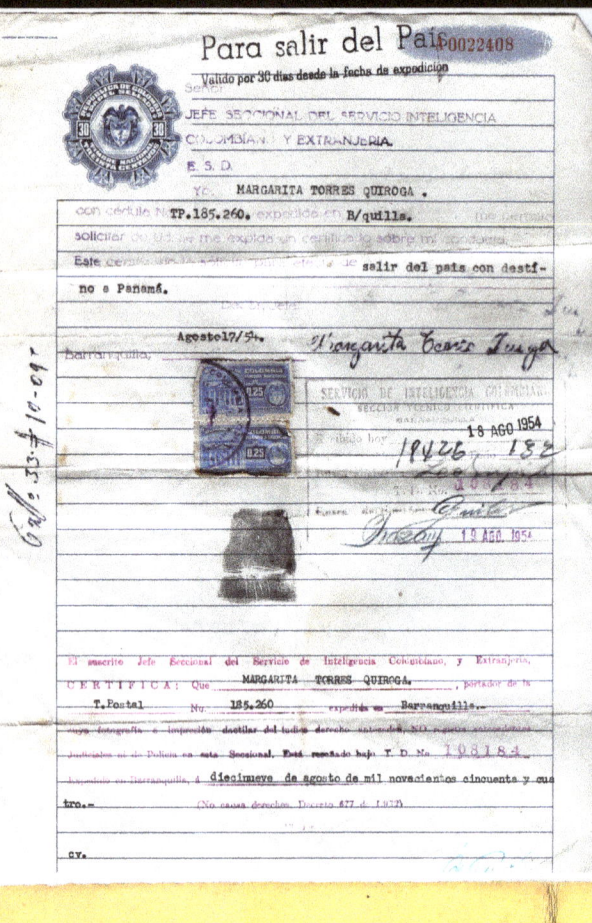

Para salir del País C0022408

Válido por 30 días desde la fecha de expedición

JEFE SECCIONAL DEL SERVICIO INTELIGENCIA
COLOMBIANA Y EXTRANJERIA.
E.S.D.

Yo. MARGARITA TORRES QUIROGA.
con cédula No TP.185.260. expedida en B/quilla.

Agosto 17/54
Barranquilla,

18 AGO 1954

CERTIFICA: Que MARGARITA TORRES QUIROGA,
T. Postal No. 185.260 expedida en Barranquilla.

diecinueve de agosto de mil novecientos cincuenta y cuatro.

CONSTE

QUE la SEÑORITA MARGARITA TORRES QUIROGA.

ha pasado el examen correspondiente ante la Junta de
Censura de Espectáculos Públicos de Colón y clasificad.. como
ARTISTA.

Colón, 3 de Feb. de 195 5

El Gobernador,

Presidente de la Junta

El Secretario

Carnet No 119

Nacionalidad: Colombiana
Color: Blanca
Edad: 25 años
Pelo: Lacio Negro
Ojos: Pardos
Cédula: Peru) Boga
Estado Civil: Soltera
Señas particulares: Ninguna

Firma del Artista,

NOTA: Devuélvase este Carnet al abandonar el país.

CLUB Nocturno HAPPYLAND

CHAPTER SEVEN
The Great Panamanian
Lester James Lawton

When they arrived to Colón, they immediately got booked to perform at the HappyLand night club.

One night, an apparent World Champion Arm Wrestler, after seeing Luis' STRENGTH while performing at the HappyLand night club, taunted Luis and challenged him to an arm wrestle.

The arrogant "champion" told Luis, "You may be strong, but I am a champion". Luis never backed down from any trouble makers or challenges. He agreed and sat down to arm wrestle with this apparent champion.

What transpired next was that Luis, with one arm...

One arm!...

...threw the man across several tables. The champion went flying. After a slow recovery, the champion came back toward Luis.

Luis expected a fight.

Instead, the man showed his respect for Luis' STRENGTH and apologized for his arrogance and stupidity.

After performing several times at the HappyLand night club, Luis had to face another challenge, but this one was within his own hand-to-hand balancing act!

What was happening was that Luis was Not content with the continual lover-feuds (quarrels) going on between his partner Benito and Gloria. He had tolerated the continual publicized social dramas in Colombia, but now Luis had had enough.

So Luis parted ways with Benito after he concluded this uncomfortable reality would continue.

Benito and Gloria remained in Panama for a while, but thereafter left... never to be seen again!

Weeks before Luis decided to break ties with Benito, a young 19 year old Panamanian teenager had come to see Luis and Benito rehearse before their public performances in Colón, Panama.

This young 19 year old teenager was **Lester James Lawton!**

Lester James was fascinated by the feats the duo accomplished physically. Lester James was a **young athlete** who loved life! And at his youth of 19 years of age, Lester James wanted to break free from the confines of a restrictive lifestyle.

When Luis and Benito finally separated, Luis asked Lester James if he could be the flyer. Lester James was an aspiring bodybuilder who could do, more or less, handstands on the floor. But Lester James was a quick, energetic learner and agreed.

Within a two week period, Luis had taught Lester James how to perform hand-to-hand balancing; and what followed was a hand balancing act that was hatched out in a short two week period of time! **Incredible!**

In a 2013 Interview with Lester James Lawton, the author of this illustrative book got an immediate sense of who this man was: someone with a big heart and a positive outlook on life. Additionally, Lester James was a man who overcame obstacle after obstacle, always taking care of his family as a first priority.

In Panama, young teenage Lester James chose a different path for himself, instead of that which was expected of him. Lester James wanted to venture out and take life in!
... in a physical way!
...an athletic way!

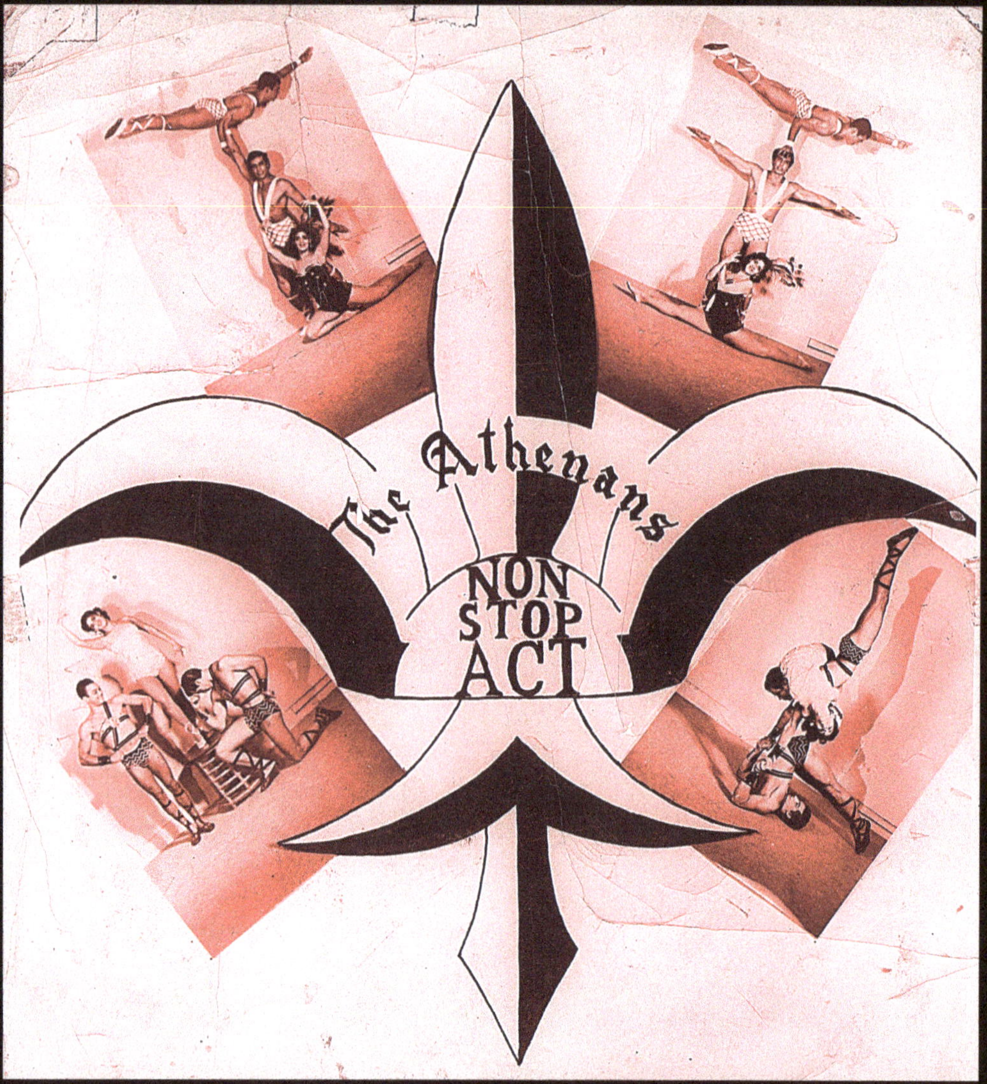
The Athenans
NON
STOP
ACT

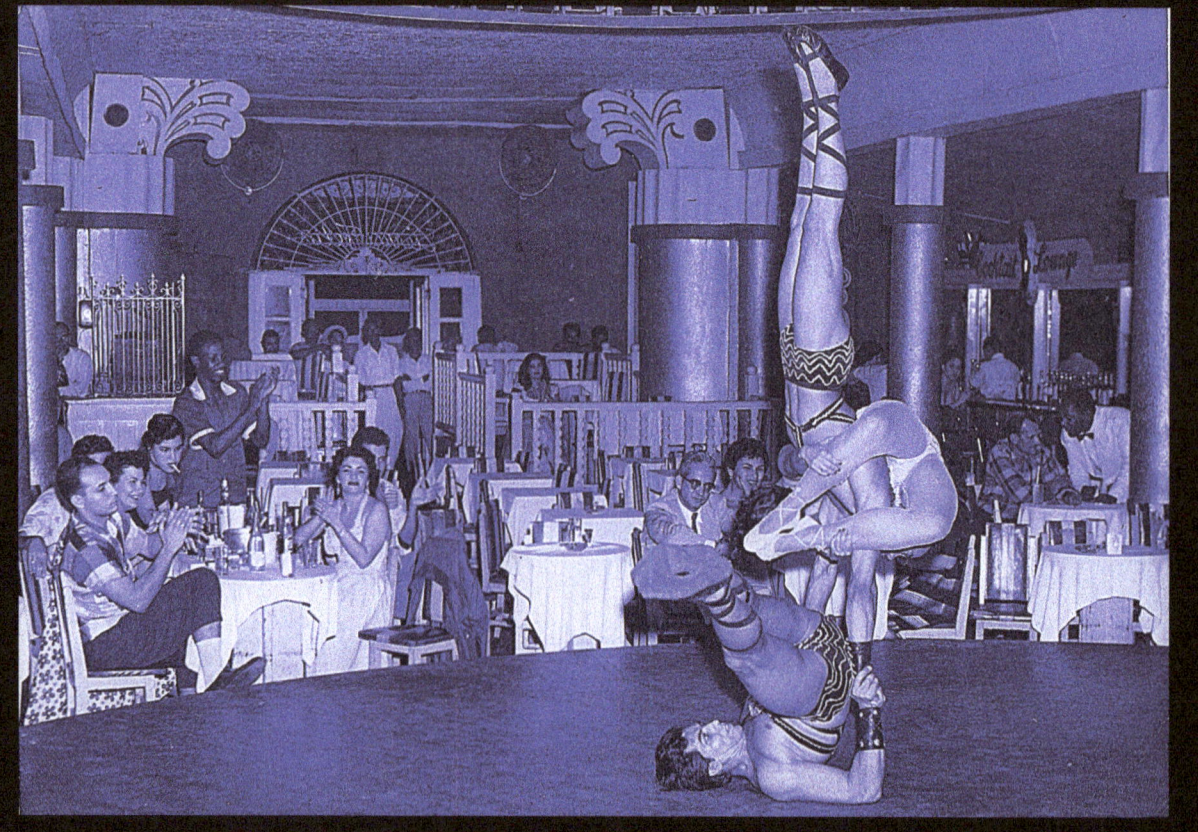

Lester James Lawton came from a wealthy Panamanian family. His mother owned a shoe store, one of his uncles owned a bakery, another uncle was an independent airline mechanic, and yet another uncle named **Harold Lawton** was in the Panamanian Secret Service.

Lester James did not like the rigidity of an upscale life...he had a maid ironing all of his clothes; and he was required to always keep his shoes shined. The culture also called for adults with adults and children with children. Since Lester James' personality is social, such restrictions were not appealing.

As to his family's origin, Lester James does not know much about where they originally came from; but he knows that his family came via Jamaica and from there Europe. His family was **Jewish**. However, when the 2nd World War came, **they changed to Catholicism because** *of the negativity imposed on* the **Jewish culture** during those times.

Lester James' mother's brother, **Abraham Lincoln Lawton**, was like a father to him; since his father no longer lived with them.

Abraham was very generous with his time and was an inspiration to Lester James Lawton.

One day, his uncle brought a bunch of body building magazines and said to Lester James, "read these". Lester James was fascinated and began body building. He was able to do a **"clean and jerk" of 550 pounds!**

His body did Not gain a GREAT VISUAL body MASS because of his body type. Nonetheless, his body was perfectly toned and his STRENGTH had increased dramatically because of the development of a bodily endurance that weightlifting demanded.

So from these beginnings, Lester James joined Luis and Margarita in their hand balancing act. They kept their previous name, but in the English wording, "The Athenians".

Because Lester James had **an uncle in the government**, Luis and Margarita were able to stay in Panama **a year longer.**

43

It was common place to eat freshly caught fish during their days off from performing. In this Photograph, Margarita is preparig fish caught by Luis and Lester James!

Enjoying a Costa Rican pool, Little five year old Rosie Clings to Luis and Margarita. Lester James enjoying the outdoors and the people of this country! Photograph below left: Luis as Flyer and Margarita as Base in a Costa Rican Beach:)

Luis and Lester James regularly went fishing during their time off; a pastime they both THOROUGHLY enjoyed. It was there that Lester James taught Luis how to skin dive in the ocean.

They also went underwater fishing as well! From rubber that came from tires and a stick, they created harpoons. They caught many fish by way of harpooning under water!

They both enjoyed each other's company.

Lester James recalls that they would eat loads of food and not gain an ounce of fat since the regular, arduous training that came with hand-to-hand balancing would consume a lot of the energy they ate. So there was no need for a special diet since their physical activities demanded much physical energy.

Although they started a hand-to-hand balancing act quickly, it took Lester James about **3 months to perfect the required positioning and maintenance of this physical art form.**

In particular, Luis constantly emphasized that both bodies needed to be "locked" **as one** while in a hand-to-hand balancing position. This emphasis of locking proved itself to be a key component for a successful execution in front of an audience.

Since Lester James Lawton was also lifting weights at the same time, Luis told him he needed to reduce this activity. Lester James' muscles would not lock completely into a successful hand balancing position because of the buildup of muscle around key body areas responsible for a good **"locking"** of his own body with that of Luis'.

So Lester James began to minimize his weight lifting in order to perfect the required locking position required for a successful hand-to-hand balancing act.

Lester James vividly recalls that Luis was **very patient with him**...and his patience paid off!!! Lester James BECAME a great flyer!!!

As they performed in Colón and Panama City, Luis and his wife-to-be (Margarita) would constantly hustle to look for gigs, since they did not have an agent. Finding work was not always easy.

As with any type of performance endeavor, in those days, and even in these days, unless one was/is well connected, work was and is Not consistent; and that gaining any sort of monetary success is limited; especially for performers without agents or inexperienced in successfully running a profitable business.

This lack of agent did not hamper the spirits of Luis, Lester James, and Margarita who loved what they set out to do.

Luis, according to Lester James, was **ALWAYS talking about hand balancing**. It truly was an art form Luis loved and cherished deeearly.

After about a year, in 1955, the trio headed north to Costa Rica: where they were able to work for 2 months.

The country that followed was Nicaragua at the Teatro Margot in Managua. At this theater, the famous Mexican Actress María Félix had performed at the same event as theirs. The trio performed right after her number at this theater.

The beauty of Nicaragua, with its volcanos, lakes, lagoons, beaches, and people, captivated the trio. This is as far as Lester had ever traveled (as was also true for Margarita who had never left South America prior to going to Panama).

The Teatro Margot in Managua as of 2022 lies in ruins following a devastating earthquake and civil unrest of the 1970's. So as with all things in this world, nothing lasts!

But the memories of those who performed there will live on forever...as out of these bodies we are eternal! J.

45

Para mi querido Padrecito Adán Q.

Con una típico Guatemalteca y la
Catedral de Quetzaltenango 2ª
Capital de Guatemala · 4-17-56

Para mi Abuelito Adán Arrizaga

Apagando las Velas de mi Cumpleaños en Guatemala País de la Maravillosa Raza Maya.

In Nicaragua, Lester James met a beautiful Nicaragüense by the name of Berta (a hairstylist who owned a salon where Margarita went to have her hair done). Lester James fell in love with Berta. Lester, being a handsome performer with a great physique and an attractive set of blue eyes, had many women seeking his attention. But, this woman Berta captivated him.

However, travel was the life of a performer; and off Lester James and the rest of the trio went. They had spent several months in Nicaragua. And his beloved Nicaragüense stayed.

Their next country stop was Guatemala, Central America. Luis had been advised that there was a circus that may need an act there. While Luis and Margarita went looking for this circus in Guatemala City, Lester James became the caregiver of five-year-old Rosie, daughter of Margarita.

When they located the circus, it was nothing more than a group of mediocre acts around an open air "redonda" or "pista de circo" or "ring" where performances were executed. The circus had failed financially and it was struggling to stay in business.

Luis and Margarita proposed to help the circus owners improve the circus. The circus owners accepted the help. Luis and Margarita were experienced tenured circus performers who had been to various types of circuses, big and small. After Luis and the rest of the trio entered the circus, they improved the line-up of the performances. Then they focused on the propaganda to BRING IN in audiences to **Circo Blanca Elizabeth**.

The trio's act was at the end of the show since it was the best one. The new campaign brought in many circus goers. The next steps taken were to construct a circus performance tent. That task was carefully accomplished as well with many hands!

Previous Page Upper Left Photograph:....Margarita sends this photograph to her father in Colombia. It reads, "For my loving Father Adan Q. I am here with a typical Guatemalteca (Guatemalan) and the Cathedral of Quetzaltenango..2nd Capital of Guatemala 4-17-56." Quetzaltenango's indigenous name is Xelajú. It is locally called Xela. Quetzaltenango is the second largest city in Guatemala with about 61% Indigenous people. It is a valley that borders a huge mountain range.

Previous Relevent photograph: Rosie hitting the Piñata with children from the circus her parents are helping.

Right Middle: Margarita Exploring the Beauty of Guatemala

Previous Page Upper Right Photograph: Margarita and family Exploring Guatemala! On this occassion, little Rosie is celebrating her Birthday of Six years old on April 13, 1956.

As months passed, the popularity of the circus began to grow and they were able to buy two trucks to transport the gear from one town to the next.

And it was in this circus that Lester James found his future wife, Julieta Elizabeth; daughter of the circus owners.

When Luis felt it was time to move on to Mexico, Lester James had second thoughts. He was in love with Julieta and wanted to continue to help the circus. Luis wanted to perform in Mexico and eventually in the United States. However, it became evident that Lester James would stay; his mind was set.

So Lester James stayed and made a hand balancing act with Julieta, who became his wife and the mother of his children.

In retrospect, Margarita tells the author of this book (her first grandson) that if Luis had stayed with Benito, had a little patience with the situation, that they would have continued performing. And that, eventually, they would have gone to the places Luis wanted to go and perform at: The United States of America, Canada, and Europe.

Far Right: Lester James remembers that while doing this one-arm handstand, he heard the two men to the right middle of the photograph conversing that if he had not placed his weight equally, Julieta would have broken her neck! They were both medical doctors.

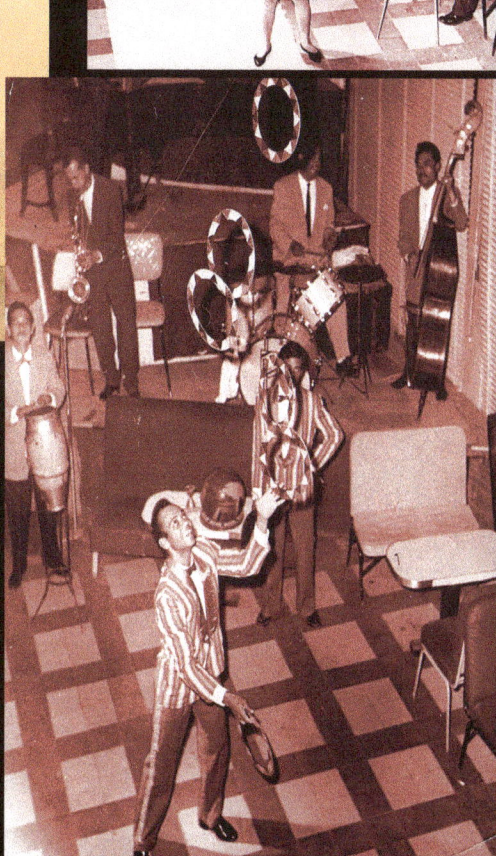

In order to make extra income, Lester learned other circus skills such as juggling.

On this page we see him in action! As seen, he also performed in nightclubs in addition to the Blanca Elizabeth circus. A very dedicated man!

49

Little Rosie practicing handstands in 1956 in Juarez, Mexico, in the little shed like area given to them as accomodations when they first arrived to this border city. Life was difficult, but they made the best of the circumstance.

Luis' and Margaritas' first job was to make and sell wooden puppets! *Jay Park Origin Image Pixaby Free Use: Modification: D.Darseli Santana*

Margarita observes her daughter Rosie do a handstand in their one-room home when they arrived in Juarez, Chihuahua in 1956.

CHAPTER 8
Farewell to Guatemala

Kon'nichiwa
こんにちは

JUAREZ!

In September of 1956, Luis, Margarita, and little Rosie departed by train from Guatemala in route to an "unknown" in Mexico. They traveled through Chiapas where Margarita saw, for the first time, topless native women! She was surprised at this display, not knowing that in certain cultures it is common place to be without a top.

On September 16th, Mexico's Independence Day, they arrived at the country's capital of Mexico City.

The couple had very limited resources, and the money was running out!

Margarita was pregnant with Luis' first son, Francisco. She became pregnant in Nicaragua. Margarita had saved money in Guatemala to pay a clinic for the childbearing costs; but now that money was needed for their transportation needs. Hence, their situation was becoming precarious.

While in Mexico City, Margarita wanted Luis to seek help of accommodations and food from his former comrades: the Lucas family. Luis however felt it was not right since the couple were not married. Erroneously Luis put a rigid culture mindset in front of mitigating necessity the young acrobatic family was experiencing.

Without contacting the Lucas family, and after a couple of days in the country's capital, the acrobatic family headed to Luis' home state of Michoacán by bus and stayed with relatives. It was there that Luis and Margarita legally wed.

Their stay in Michoacán was meant to be temporary; and so they were there for only about a week and a half.

Margarita suggested that they try to go to the United States of America via first making a home in a U.S.-Mexico border town. At that time, there were many trains heading to Juarez, Mexico. As such, they chose Juarez as their springboard to the United States.

At a Michoacán train station, Luis purchased three train tickets, second class, destined to **Juarez, Chihuahua, Mexico**...the border town with the U.S. **sister city of El Paso, Texas**.

At the train station they were escorted to first class since they were well dressed and were thought to be financially rich people. However, when the time of ticket call came, they were forced to move to 2nd class.

When they arrived in Juarez, they were...

dead poor!

Margarita recalls that when they arrived to the train depot in Juarez, they only had the equivalent of a U.S. dollar in their pocket.

The money had run out!

Margarita, being the social person that she was and is, on the train made a friendship with a woman who lived in Juarez but worked in El Paso. This woman, seeing that they were well dressed and acrobatic performers, offered them a tiny shed like room in back of her home in Juarez.

Since they had no other choice, the couple readily and gratefully accepted!

Juarez Night Life Scene photograph and Myra Taylor photograph are Depictions Only, Representing them during the time when Luis Pimentel Ruiz and Family had been in Juarez in the late 1950's

The first couple of months Luis and Margarita worked for a man making and selling puppet clowns! They were paid for every dozen of them they sold on the street.

Luis had decided that his performance days were to be limited without a reliable flyer, and since now he needed some sort of regular stable income to support his wife, little Rosie, and now Francisco who was on his way. His commitment to slow down was genuine.

In October of 1956, when a circus came to Juarez, Luis went and immediately noticed some acrobats who he knew when he first started off in Mexico...**the Gaona brothers: Mario and Raul Gaona.** They agreed to make a trio hand balancing act while in Juarez with Luis. All being athletes, they hatched out a hand-to-hand balancing act and performed that very night! However, the partnership lasted about two weeks and then the circus moved on. They urged Luis to go; but Luis needed to be with his wife who was soon to give birth to their son.

The times had changed.

The Gaona family later joined the **Ringling Brothers and Barnum and Bailey Circus** as successful trapeze artists known as the "Flying Gaonas"! They were under the guidance of **Victor Gaona.**

During the night Luis and Margarita would go to the then 1950's glamorous nightclubs of Ciudad Juarez. They went to see if they would find anyone Luis possibly knew from times of past; maybe someone who could offer Luis a better, more stable occupation within that region of Texas-Chihuahua.

They also went into these clubs to sell their numerous artistic outfits since they needed the money for sustenance!

And luck found its way!

It turned out that in one of those night clubs an African American singer named **Myra Taylor** became friends with Margarita. Myra lived in El Paso while she performed in Juarez.

The Juarez nightclubs in this era where bringing in American entertainers to entertain large American audiences that frequently crossed the border to have some fun!

The American Prohibition Era of the 1920's and early 1930's made Juarez a place to get entertainment; when restrictions on liquor made it impossible to have a cup of joy!

And so, the crossing-the-border tradition that had developed during this prohibition period **remained strong when the 1950's came along.**

The Jazz singer Myra Taylor, out of compassion, hired Margarita to help her with her household chores. Little Rosie would go and pretend play that she was fashioning Myra's hair and putting on her make-up!

Myra treated Margarita as family.

In those days, the border was easy to cross with "day passes" issued to locals from both Juarez and El Paso.

One of Myra's El Paso friends, **Kay McNaughton**, was also very kind to Margarita. She would bring her clothes and food during her pregnancy.

It was **Kay's husband Mac** (owner of an El Paso construction company) that gave Luis his first break at a better job!

It was this generous family that **pulled Luis and his family out of poverty.**

Luis was a fast learner and soon became a very competent commercial taper and painter.

Mac and Kay had two children: Liza and David McNaughton, who became playmates to Luis' and Margarita's children.

It was also the McNaughton's that helped Luis get his immigration papers to live in the United States.

Luis worked hard as a construction worker and traveled quite a bit in the United States working under McNaughton and later with other employers. One trip took him to a year in Alaska! While there, he sent money back to Juarez to care for his family. He also stayed a while in Kansas and Georgia. In Georgia, a military officer offered him an apartment so that he could bring his family while he was there. The military officer was married to a Puerto Rican woman who was also very kind. Margarita has fond memories of the great hospitality they received from this couple and their children.

Thereafter, Luis worked for 23 other construction businesses that hired him because of his attention to detail. Some of these included Basin Builders Corporation, and Paramount Painting, both in Los Angeles; Commercial Drywall Contractors Inc.; and Rutherford, Inc. These were just a few he worked for under the union, but some of the work was non-union.

Luis with his boss, Mr. Johnny McNaughton, in Alsaka in the late 1950s.

53

Margarita, Little Francisco Pimentel, Luis' son, who was born in Juarez, Mexico on November 2, 1956. Little Rosie Smiling at her cute little brother. As can be seen from their clothing, they are doing much better financially then when they initially arrived to Juarez. Luis had already begun working in construction in the United States and so things became more tolerable. Luis was frequently traveling the country on job assignments which put some stress on their marriage. But, they overcame!

On this page and the following, Luis Pimentel Ruiz at an Alaskan festival event in the late 1950s. He had spent a year there working during a construction gig. He often played his guitar during his time off and did a good number of sight seeing expeditions. As can be seen, he kept a physical regimen that maintained his strength. He held hope that one day he would be able to resume hand-balancing.

Right image: Kay McNaughton with her two children Liza and David. At the center Rosie, her mother and brother.

Margarita is making a serious face for reasons that will not be disclosed in this book; but will be revealed in the future publication of her detailed life story to be written by the author of this book.

Kay and her husband really were great people! They got out of their way to help out a family. A great example for all human beings to follow! As a society, in 2022, we have lost this commitment to community. Hopefully, we can organize in our community to bring value to community over corporations (and other self-interst groups) and individuals. And hopefully the g o v e r n m e n t s can be more responsive to community too.

Let's do our part...yes you and I do our parts.

Luis, during his time off, would also indulge in other interests of his; such as playing the guitar and singing. He became fluent in the instrument and was frequently playing songs of old in the Spanish language; romantic songs! Margarita would come at times and sing with him. She has a beautiful high pitch voice that complemented his tenor voice.

Circa 1964, Luis in Georgia at a military installation. His wife was able to join him during his work their because of the generous military family who offered them an apartment. Pictured are teenage Rosie, the Puerto Rican wife of the military officer. Little

Left: Luis in late 1961 holding the new addition to the family, Janet Pimentel Quiroga born January 9, 1961 in El Paso, Texas. Francisco looks on! The site is in Juarez, where Luis is building additions to a property the family bought.

Being an excellent "base", Luis skillfully holds his daughter in balance even before she is able to walk!

Below left: The New Family Enjoying a stroll in the streets of Juarez in 1964. Little Janet looking at a curious boy!

And The Family Story Begins In Santa Monica, California in 1965!

Above is a man who lived with Luis and his family. Since he was living by himself and in need of company, Luis welcomed him into his home.

The man was a mute with a monkey. His name was Virgilio. His prior occupation is unknown. Luis was still travelling around the country. However, when he discovered Santa Monica, California, he made it a point to take work only within a 100 mile radius. He had enough influence in his talent as a painter and taper to make this desire to stay close to home a reality!

CHAPTER NINE
1960's
The Pimentel Family at Muscle Beach
Santa Monica, California

One of Luis' employers took him to Santa Monica California in 1963.

Luis immediately fell in love with this southern beach city; especially with its athletic environment at Muscle Beach. He knew that this is where he wanted to be!

The Santa Monica bug had stung Luis Pimentel Ruiz!

He became hooked!

Therefore, in late July of 1965, at the age of 44, having bought a house in Juarez, he sold it, and moved Margarita and the family all to Santa Monica, California; three blocks from the Ocean on the corner of Hill and 3rd Street. This is the date that officially marks his stay in California with his wife and children. He had been there two years earlier working, but alone without his family.

The family had grown and now included the two additions to the family: Francisco Pimentel, born November 2, 1956 in Juarez, Mexico (conceived in Nicaragua); and Janet Pimentel, born in 1961, in El Paso, Texas (conceived in Juarez). Maria Rosario (Rosie) Martínez Quiroga was now turning 15 years old in 1965!

Once settled, it was a ritual that after Luis finished construction work at around 2:30 p.m. on any given day, the entire family walked down to the beach and spent the rest of their daylight hours exercising acrobatics and having barbeque fish! **This was done every single day!**

The beach became their front patio!

Life was exciting for all in the family during this time. Margarita Pimentel got her beautician license and became a hair stylist at a local beauty salon. Luis trained Rosie in hand-to-hand balancing.

Thereafter, Luis and Rosie made a hand balancing act which they performed.

The "Flyer" known as "El Niño" or "Kid Alfredo Reyes" shown on this page was a professional Hand Balancer they met, along with his wife Eva, at Muscle Beach in Santa Monica in 1965. Luis would have loved to have professonally perform with this Cuban Athlete, but Alfredo Reyes already had a Las Vegas act with another "Base". Prior to the act in Vegas, Alfredo had artistic contracts in other countries such as in South Africa.

Kid Alfredo Reyes was injured in a car accident in Vegas and became paralyzed circa 1968. His son Ulises followed in his artistic footsteps and a became a "Flyer" as well. Later both son Ulises and daughter Sonia opened their own successful Hair Salons in Las Vegas.

Margarita, shown acrobatically performing in this page, became friends with Eva also a beautician: in Las Vegas. They had an apartment not too far from Santa Monica, shown in the picture. Their regular home town was Vegas since that is where Kid Alfredo Reyes performed regularly. The family remains in Las Vegas to this day.

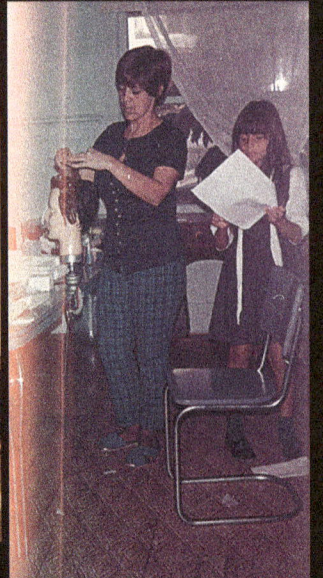

Summer of 1967, Luis Pimentel Ruiz and Rosie Martinez Quiroga Torres Perform During a Photo Shoot Sponsored by Luis in Preparations for a Professional Run.

But in June of 1967, at the age of 17 years of age, Rosie became pregnant with her first son (the author of this book) and that ended the ambitions Luis had of going to Las Vegas and performing regularly with Rosie.

In the artistic photo-shoot Luis made of their act, presented in this book, Rosie is about 3 months pregnant!

But artistic hope for Luis was on the horizon!

In 1969, Luis was given a surprise of a lifetime!

At Muscle Beach, the Panamanian Lester James Lawton appeared! It turns out that after 7 years in Guatemala, Lester and his wife went to Panama, where Lester James was able to obtain a Visa to move to the United States. Life in a small Central American circus was difficult: setting up the tent and breaking it down in every town; and living in a trailer had many issues as well. So, when Julieta became pregnant with their first child Sylvia, they decided it was time for a new life!

And since Lester James was an acrobatic athlete and living in Los Angeles County, it was only natural for him to gravitate to Muscle Beach: where at the time it was the **goto place to workout** in a beautiful beach environment. And hence, both Luis and Lester James gravitated to the same place to work out in Santa Monica, California!

Luis was very excited about restarting the hand-to-hand balancing act with Lester James which had ended in Guatemala. They did begin rehearsing every day in McArthur Park, near were Lester James lived initially (thereafter Lester James bought a home in Culver City).

The duo performed at this park a few times and at Luis' Venice High School graduation ceremony on Tuesday, June 3, 1969.

Luis had returned to school via the adult school program of the **Los Angeles Unified School District** to complete his high school education. And he did this while working full time!

However, the duo was short lived since Lester James had already made plans with a Cuban man by the name of Angel Llaurado. Angel acquired the acrobatic services of Lester James because Angel's prior hand balancing act called **Rola and Roland** with "the flyer" **Kid Alfredo Reyes** ended because the "Kid" permanently broke his back in a car accident and was not able to continue performing. Hence, Angel was looking for a replacement flyer and hired Lester James.

Lester James Lawton (Flyer)

Angel Llaurado (Middle Base)

Luis Pimentel Ruiz (Principal Base)

63

The duo of Angel Llaurado and Lester James Lawton, as Rola and Roland, lasted about 3 years, where they performed at many venues across the country regularly. However, Lester had disagreements with Angel. Lester James felt strongly that regular rehearsal (practice) was essential in order to keep form and to avoid injury. This was a rule Luis Pimentel Ruiz had taught Lester James back in Colón, Panama.

So, because of this continual disagreement between Lester James and Angel, Lester bid farewell to the World of Acrobatics when their contract expired with their agent.

From that point on, Lester focused his attention to his wife, Julieta, and their five children. He had a regular job as a truck driver at the docks, working for the **Yellow Trucking Company**; so he was fine with leaving behind a life of uncertainty that comes with performing.

So the first acrobatic offshoot of Luis Pimentel Ruiz had called it quits.

Divergently, Luis Pimentel Ruiz made No such call for himself!

Luis' passion for this art form actively **continued Continuously for an additional 34 years from this 1969 point in time!!!!**

CHAPTER TEN
Luis Pimentel Ruiz
And
MUSCLE BEACH
Santa Monica, California
1970'S TO 1990'S

With Lester James parting ways from Luis (again!), Luis was left without a flyer. Luis wanted so much to continue the art form that he loved. He did momentarily meet with Dario Lucas and during the early 1970's he continued on professionally for a while as discussed in the introduction of this book. After the artistic short-lived era of Dario Lucas (as explained earlier), Luis never again professionally performed hand-to-hand balancing because of the lack of a regular flyer.

Notwithstanding, Luis' passion continued on at **Muscle Beach**, California: where he regularly trained enthusiasts, and where he participated in creating and performing on-the-spot hand-to-hand balancing acts with those who shared his spirit and love for this physical art form.

To The Right and In the Following Pages: Jose Dario Lucas (Flyer) and Luis Pimentel Ruiz (Base) performing the acrobatic Art of Hand Balancing.

When Rosie arrived in 1965, Rosie would baby sit right near her home on third and hill in Santa Monica..

THE
★ ★ ★
"AMERICANS"
★ ★ ★ ★ ★ ★ ★

65

THE
☆ ☆ ☆ ☆
"AMERICANS"
☆ ☆ ☆ ☆ ☆ ☆ ☆

The Mexican Athletes Luis Pimentel Ruiz and Dario Lucas performed professionally during the early and mid 1970's. These Americans from Mexico brought Marvel to the United States of America!

The Americans

And on March 7th of 1968, Rosie became a mom! Right: Rosie, Margarita, and the author of this book at age 1...pictured on Hill and 3rd Street in October of 1969.

Above, Luis and Peter Morales (Massachusettes Film Editor and Producer, and Margarita's nephew) along the Palisades Park in Santa Monica in 1973.

Below during the same time is from Left to Right: Francisco Pimentel, Peter Morales, Jose Maria Pimentel (Luis' father), Janet Pimentel and Luis.

Luis made a special trip to Michoacán, with Margarita, to pick up his father who was now very old and in need of attention. The author of this book remembers this man as very gentle. He would give Rosie's kids a few cents so that they could go and get candy and gum at a mini mart that existed near the corner of Main Street and Hill.

Above: The First Grandson of Luis Pimentel Ruiz (the author of this book) contemplates life as he walks along the shore just North West of Hill Street in May 1970.

This child has been contemplative from Birth to the Present. For decades it felt like a curse: the mind being opened continuously to that which is beyond this world; on a *daily basis* feeling as a foreigner to this existence called life. But now, that which was not understood is understood! J

69

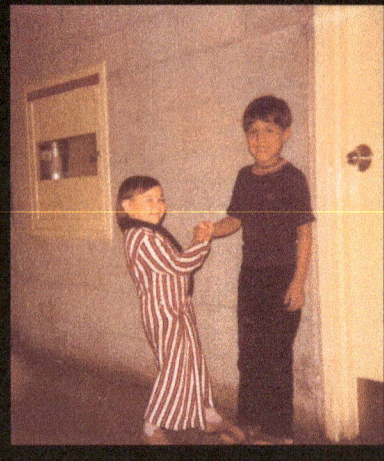

Left: the author of this book at one of the frequent visits to Ringling Brothers and Barnum and Bailey Circus. Also in the picture is the *then* "smallest man on Earth", Mihaly "Michu" Meszaros from Budapest, Hungary. He measures slightly less than 3 feet tall. Apparently, there is now an even smaller adult!

The author remembers seeing Michu's wife: a beautiful tall, blond woman!

Below Middle: The author of this book with his younger brother, William Soto (by column), sitting on the porch of Luis' home in 1974 (3rd St. & Hill).

Below Last Image: April 1972 image of Steven Maurice Soto, Rosie's last and youngest son; enjoying viewing vehicles passing by. Behind him: the **Big Blue Bus** I remember as a child!

The 1970s In California

Naked people on the beach, Walking
as if clothed!

Rigid and Religious Politicians Seeking to Exercise Power

Colorful Stripes and Growing Hair Dews!

Fuel Prices Reaching for the Stars *! ! !*

2nd Hand Stores at Every Corner

Bell-Bottoms Galore!

Dressing for the Disco of Lights

New Programming set in Music, Film,

Television, Radio,

Newsprint, Government, Business, Banks, And MORE!

...for the unhelpful Manipulation of The Minds of Children!

Religious Peoples Preaching To Go Into The Mountains
to Avoid A Pending DOOM!

And the SMELL of a T.V. Dinner!

It's All There FOLKS!

For The Taking!

[i wish i hadn't i]

D.Darseli Santana
(retrospecting the 70's as a child!)

Two athletes, out of many athletes at **Muscle Beach**, who shared this spirit and love of hand balancing with Luis Pimentel Ruiz were Cisco's **SAMOHI (Santa Monica High School)** friends **Jayme and Jarett Jamison (identical twins)**.

In the late 1970's until the 1990's, the twins were at Muscle Beach almost every day, practicing hand balancing and other acrobatic art forms.

Like many at **Muscle Beach**, the twins have a heritage of artistic achievements in their background:

The twins came from the union between their mother, the actress and dancer **Gilda Fontana**, and their Mexican father, the renowned athletic bull fighter, **Gonzalo Santos**.

It turns out that Gonzalo's father: **Gonzalo Natividad Santos Rivera**, was involved in the Mexican Revolution of 1910, and later became the Mexican Governor of **San Luis Potosí** from 1943 to 1949! Like many military men around the world, Natividad was involved in athletic extracurricular activities that inspired his son to become a renowned bull fighter.

The athlete Gonzalo the bull fighter met the athlete Gilda Fontana when she was in Mexico performing as an actress and professional flamenco dancer. The art forms met and produced **two great kids** that became athletes **stationed at Muscle Beach!**

To this day, the twins continue to challenge themselves physically. Like Luis, they fell in love with the beach culture of workouts!

The twins went off to become professionals in non-athletic trades, after attending the University of Southern California. Jarett became a successful realtor and Jayme an estate planning attorney.

Regardless of this outside activity, they keep fit and are also **Mixed Martial Arts** trainers on a part-time basis. Their love for physical endeavors **lives on!**

Jarett recalls in a late 2013 interview that Luis Pimentel was so STRONG "He could hold anyone in his hands." He further stated that **Luis was the firmest base he had ever worked with**. Jarett felt very comfortable with Luis as he held him during a hand to hand balancing workout!

Jarett further elaborates that Luis was liked by everyone at **Muscle Beach**. He recalls that one time he did drywall at their mother's house and refused to receive payment. He did it for free!

Francisco Pimentel, Luis' son, recalls that Luis always wanted to train. Another Muscle Beach enthusiast, **Patrick Tucker**, remembers Luis teaching him to always put his chest out when doing a handstand. Tucker felt comfortable learning acrobatics from Luis because of **Luis' patience to teach a new comer** into the world of acrobatics.

Red Shorts: The Twins Jarett and Jamie Jamison, Left: Ollie Thomas base and Luis Base.

71

Left:
Handstands by Jarett Jamison,
Jean-Claude Pichard, Francisco
Pimentel. Red shorts base: Jayme
Jamison, and Luis Pimentel Ruiz

Left Mid Photograph:

Handstand done by frenchman
Jean-Claude Pichard,
Luis Pimentel Base, and
Jayme Jamison

Left: Handstand participants on bar:
Ollie Thomas, Austin Moon, Francisco Pimen-
tel, Don, Jayme, Young Enthusiast in training,
Jarret. Side of bar: Jean-Claude Pichard.

In an early 2014 interview, Patrick Tucker expressed that Luis "made you want to become better at the exercise...**constantly pushing you but at the same making you feel comfortable...**"

Patrick further added, "tough, caring, and sincere best describes him..."

"you wanted to become better cause you [didn't] want to let him down...but yet he made the process fun...."

Patrick Tucker was a young lad back then. Now, **Patrick Tucker** is **a professional athletic trainer** who trains people in body building, among other physical endeavors. He also continues the art of hand to hand balancing with the twins!

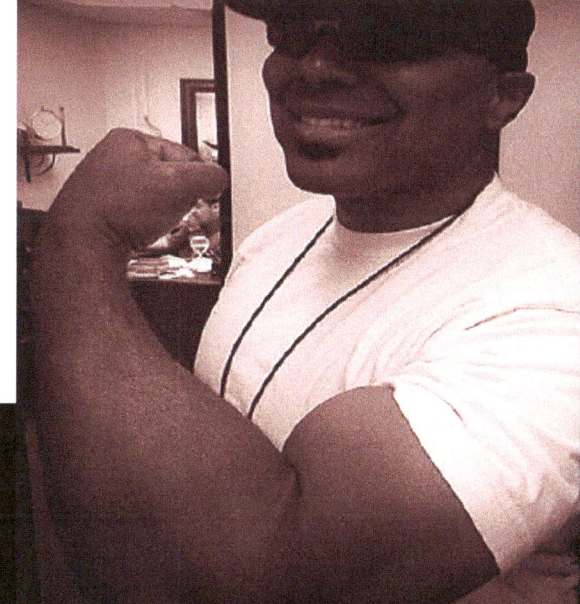

Right: Patrick Tucker, professional athletic trainer. A regular Muscle Beach athlete during Luis' time in the 80's and 90's

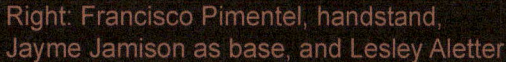

Right: Francisco Pimentel, handstand, Jayme Jamison as base, and Lesley Aletter

Above, Francisco Pimentel during a special athletic event in the 1980's at Muscle Beach. Below, Francisco as base for the female acrobat: Tricia Moon

CHAPTER ELEVEN
Cisco Pimentel
-The Acrobat!-

Luis Pimentel's enthusiasm and love for acrobatics **rubbed off** onto his son Francisco Pimentel, known as "Cisco The Kid", or just "Cisco". **Since age 2 in 1958, and up to the present year 2022**, Cisco's passion for acrobatics has not relented.

Being taught by his father hand stands, hand-to-hand balancing, and somersaults, to name a few acrobatic activities he has mastered, Cisco has, like Luis Pimentel, always kept acrobatics close to his heart. At every opportunity Francisco Pimentel has been at **Muscle Beach** practicing; and also teaching the art of acrobatics to enthusiasts from all over the world Santa Monica. Santa Monica, more than ever, has been an "international" hub for tourists from all parts of the world!

Cisco has **performed professionally** at various circuses and state fairs around the country for the **last 43 years!** He is a college educated man that prefers the open air rather than the confines of a 9 to 5 job. Like Luis, Francisco has made acrobatics his choice occupation; even though such an endeavor is mostly not always lucrative without a good agent. For Cisco the Kid, **the deep love he has for this art form is what drives him to continue performing up to this very day!**

Francisco has never done anything in his life with a premise in mind of an illusion to gain high monetary compensation. Rather, he knows how to value his time. And he has used this time to perfect his mastery of acrobatics. Joining him on his acrobatic journey is his wife, Diana Orozco (a professional certified interpreter), their three children (Francisco Jr., Diana Jr., and Christopher) and their grandchildren.

75

A

DAY

AT

MUSCLE

BEACH

CALIFORNIA

Pictured with Cisco:

1) Below: The U.S. Gold Medalist in Gymnastics: Mitch Gaylord,
who was a regular at Muscle Beach at one point.

2) In Acrobatic Attire: The Beautiful Person and Actress, Tracy Scoggins.

3) Below Mid Lft: The Beautiful Person and Actress,
Maria Conchita Alonso

4) Below Lft: The good spirited musician,
Billy Idol.

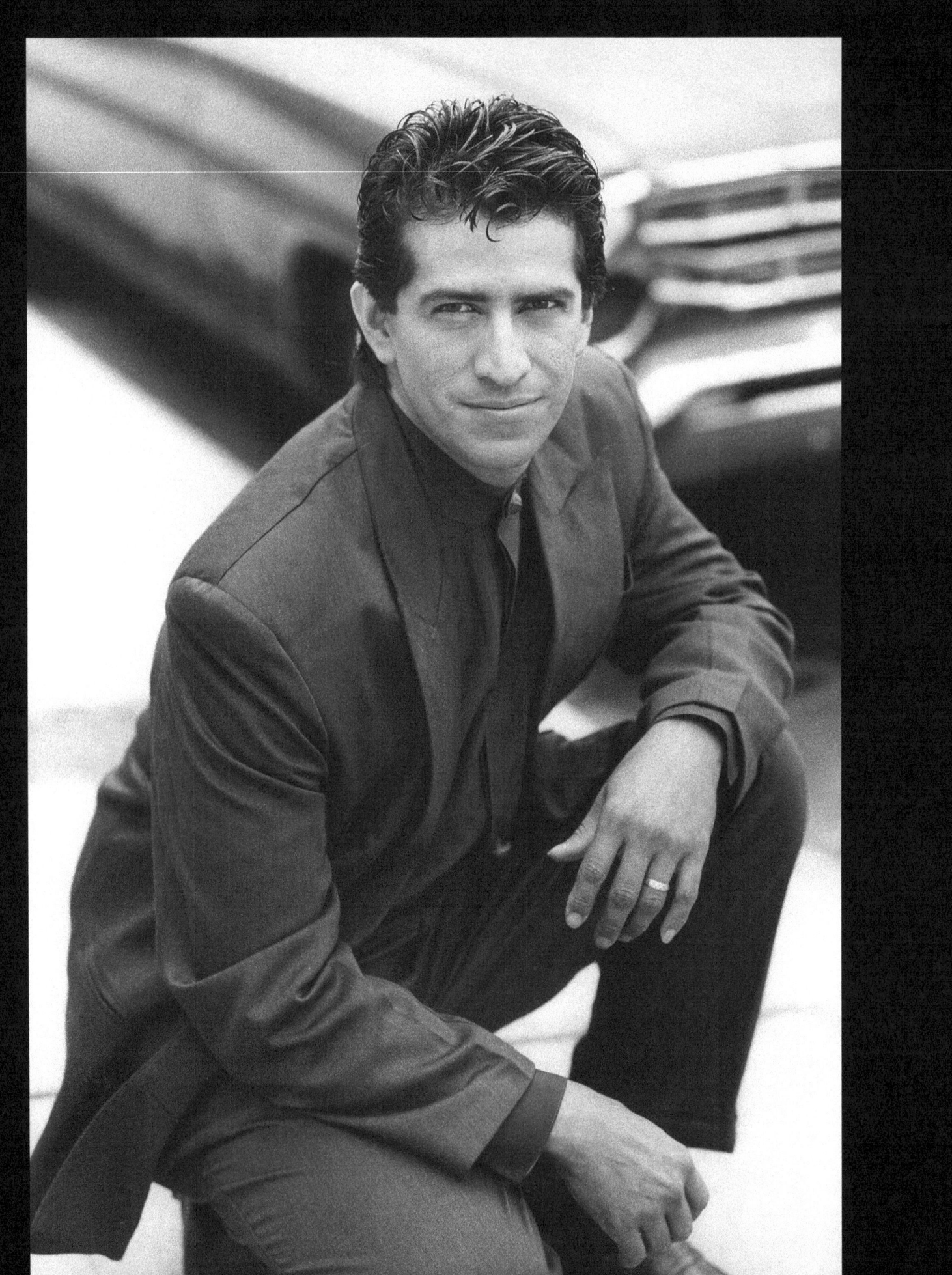

Cisco recalls how he learned acrobatics:

"My dad would have me practice at least 3 times a week. When I was very small, I would practice doing handstands against the wall." He further remembers that his father instilled on him that "being consistent" was key to dominate control over one's body in order to progress and to maintain proper form in acrobatics.

Cisco further recollects how his father Luis Pimentel taught him "back flips" in two days! Two days! "I would have a daily regimen of 10 sets of 10 back flips or handsprings, assisted by my dad"; that was a total of 100 back flips or hand springs in a day!" By the 3rd day Cisco was able to execute them by himself! **His father, Luis Pimentel Ruiz, had taught him well.**

Luis Pimentel also taught Cisco the importance of eating healthy.

And in terms of the handstand, Luis taught his son the importance of keeping toes always pointed while keeping the body firm. With that said, the author of this book, who was also taught by Luis Pimentel Ruiz, remembers the importance that was stressed by Luis in keeping shoulders slightly in front of the arms as a key to balancing correctly.

Fourteen year old Cisco being taught back flips by his father in 1970. Location, Santa Monica, California, by Bay and the Boardwalk, in a park called Cresent Bay Park with beautiful Roman Pillars and Yucca Plants on the Hills. The park was much better back in the 70's. It now seems somewhat neglected in terms on its plants and pillars. It seemed friendlier before too. Yet, it is still there! Adjacent to the park is the gran Casa Del Mar built in 1926 with Italian Style architecture by Charles F. Plummer.

Left: Francisco Pimentel and his mother Margarita at the Los Angeles Airport in the mid 1970's. He departs Santa Monica to begin his journey to Ringling Brothers and Barnum and Bailey Circus. As can be seen, his mother is very sad to see him go. Separation is always difficult for a mother.

In a late 2013 interview with Francisco Pimentel, Cisco shared that when they arrived in Santa Monica in the mid 1960's and began attending Muscle Beach every day, Luis was affectionately called by the regulars there, "Tarzan"; since he resembled the original American Tarzan, "Johnny Weissmuller". The son of this "Tarzan" was asked why he did not stay at Ringling Brother and Barnum and Bailey Circus when he attempted it in the mid 1970's to join some friends there in possibly doing trapeze work. Cisco's answer was simple: he quickly realized that this type of acrobatics was not his passion. Cisco was more interested in hand balancing. Cisco could not find someone who he could do a hand balancing act with in order to audition for the Grand show. Cisco also commented that many circus performers' take home pay, even in "Ringling", is not much; and that the government takes a good portion from their earnings!

Consequently, many performers, in order to make ends meet, wear other hats within the circus in addition to their performances; such as helpers in setting up and breaking down equipment during a circus performance, cleaning up after the animals during the show, and selling souvenirs offering them to the audience while they are in their seats or at concession stands.

Francisco says that at the circus many concession people make much more money than the performers! And in smaller circuses, the performers must also build up and break down the circus tent...an arduous task.

Cisco states that now big shows now like Cirque du Soleil are better for performers: they get paid more and usually do only 1 or 2 shows a night, instead of 3. Luis Pimentel Ruiz did 3 shows daily when he traveled with circuses in Mexico, Central America, and South America.

Francisco also commented that in these current type shows, performers do not need to do extra work because of the better pay. But regardless, in other medium to small size circuses, the difficulties to make ends meet continue to this day!

These physical circus performers, like Luis Pimentel Ruiz and his son Cisco, continue their acrobatic art form because it is a passion deep inside their hearts! J.

Below: Francisco doing a handstand at an amusement park. The author of this book (left wearing a brown leather jacket), and friend Juan Conchas (right with jacket and white shirt) looks on in admiration. Cisco would do handstands everywhere he could find an opportunity to do one! He often would go on very tall house inclined-roof-tops and do one!

Above: Francisco doing a handstand on top of a soccer goal stand! Location: Marine Park on Marine Street, Santa Monica, California.

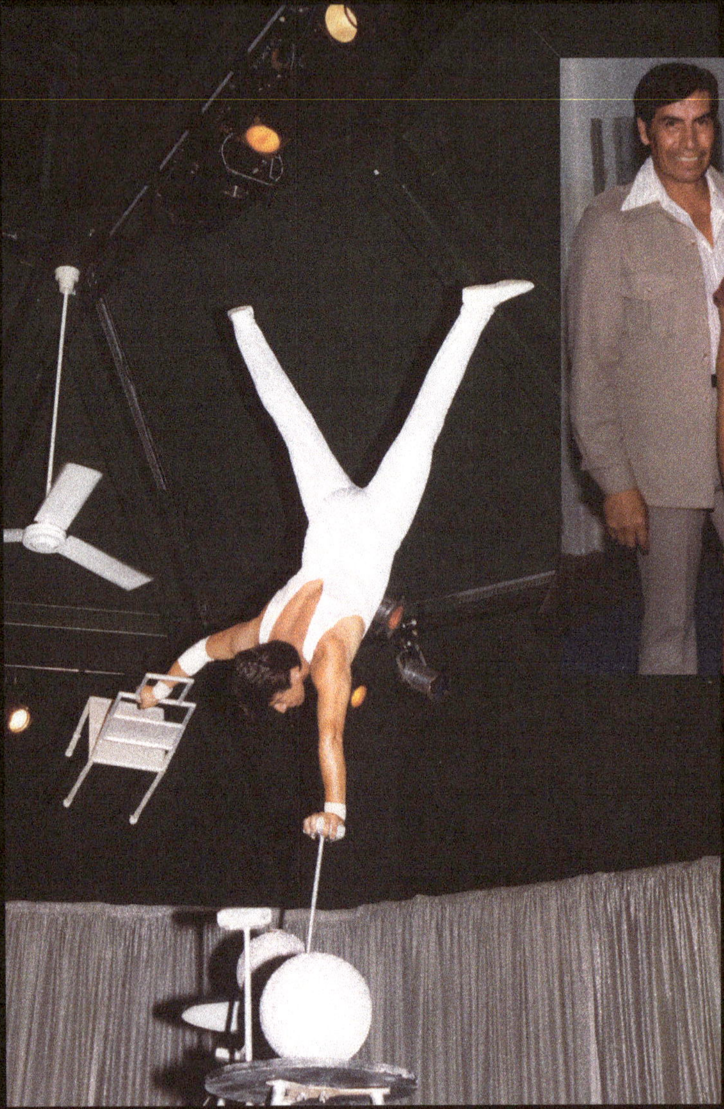

Above: Luis Pimentel Ruiz visiting Ringling Brothers and Barnum and Baily Circus. Also pictured is Muscle Beach founding member, Paula Boelsems (center woman standing), and more Acrobatic Friends!

Left: Francisco with another great athlete and acrobat: the great **Harold Lloyd Nicholas**.

Harold was a world famous tap dancer who had an act with his brother Fayard Antonio Nicholas. The brother's duo was called, the "Nicholas Brothers". Their first appearance was at The Cotton Club in New York City in the early 1930s.

Their Extraordinary versatility the brothers had as dancers made them well known. To this day, only a few can reach the heals of such greatness in dance that the brothers exhibited! They were truly dedicated to their acrobatic art form!

85

CHAPTER TWELVE
Luis Pimentel's Later Years
Santa Monica, California

During his continued acrobatic training of hand balancing, Luis continued his day job of taper and painter. After retirement, Luis gave his time to many groups of people: including serving as a volunteer for many years at **Santa Monica High School (SAMOHI).**

Luis Pimentel Ruiz worked at the **SAMOHI** records department, having the analytical skills to keep all records in logical and quick reference order.

Because of his excellence in volunteer work at **SAMOHI**, the director of the records department urged the district to pay him a stipend for his continual work. Luis said no. However, the entire staff insisted he accept and he did so accept a stipend as a show of appreciation for his years of service.

Before his retirement, Luis Pimentel took the time to teach mathematics and astronomy to his adopted grandchildren: David (the author of this book), Steven Maurice, and William. I remember Luis coming consistently with his white chalk and portable large green chalk board to teach us the very basics we still use today! Although we did not want to learn, he kept coming and we learned to appreciate his effort and the knowledge he instilled in us. He also took the time to play sports with us, including basketball. Luis encouraged us to pursue athletic activities we enjoy doing. Luis Pimentel Ruiz truly served as a grandfather we never knew. And for that, I write this book!

Luis believed in the power of knowledge and was always reading.

His favorite subjects were chemistry and astronomy. Whenever any of his grandchildren had a question on a star in the heavens, Luis knew right away the name of the star and what was known about it. Luis knew the names of stars and planets that were out at any particular time of the year!

Hand balancing continued in Luis' later years **WITHOUT RELENT!!!** Son Francisco recalls that at age 67, Luis Pimentel Ruiz held and pressed up a 212 pound African American athlete by the name of Ollie (Ali) Thomas at **Muscle Beach.** His STRENGTH was still there!!!!

And this continued into his early 80's!! Luis Pimentel Ruiz could still competently hold "flyers" in his hands even after he was diagnosed with   prostate cancer, and after two operations!

Santa Monica-Malibu Unified School District
1651 Sixteenth Street, Santa Monica, California 90404-3891 • (310) 450-8338 • Fax (310) 450-1667

May 13, 1994

Luis Pimentel
100 Marine Street
Santa Monica, CA 90405

Dear Luis:

I want to take this opportunity to thank
you for all the support you provide to
Santa Monica High School assisting with
records. The time you generously give
to help the staff accomplish their daily
responsibilities is an extremely valuable
contribution.

Thank you for enhancing the lives of the
staff and students of our District. Your
efforts are very much valued and
appreciated.

Sincerely,

Neil Schmidt
Superintendent

NS:jmw

Dr. Neil Schmidt, Superintendent of Schools

CALIFORNIA CONGRESS OF PARENTS, TEACHERS, AND STUDENTS, INC.

Honorary Service Award

presented to

Luis Pimentel

*for recognition of outstanding service to children and youth.
This contribution to the Honorary Service Award Program Fund enables the
California State PTA to provide scholarships for students and individuals
to further their education,
as well as grants for Units, Councils and Districts.*

Presented by Santa Monica High School PTSA, Inc.   Date 03/26/01

State President *Lavonne McBroom*   No. 260048

The author of this book remembers Luis' love for
birds. He frequently had a crowd of pigeons come
to his home and feed. In fact, he fed them every
single day and had names for
each of them which he could
identify! In the picture above,
he is feeding the seagulls on a
clear day in Santa Monica. Luis
also spent time with two of 3
of his youngest granchildren.
Pictured are Cisco's kids: Diana
Jr. and Cisco Jr.!

Above: Luis celebrating the marriage
between his grandson William and
Yasmin

Right: The youngest of Francisco Pimentel's children is:
Christopher "Chris" Pimentel
Orozco. Chris became the
most enthusiastic family member besides Cisco and Luis to
pursue the love of acrobatics
through the vehicle of Gymnastics. Chris dedicated all
of his childhood to that which
requires much discipline and
enthusiasm to acheive excellence, which he has! Mar-
garita Pimentel Quiroga Torres
shares in a moment of Chris'
acrobatic recognition acheiv-
ments in this photo.

87

Standing at 6 feet 8 inches tall, a former Santa Monica High School football player, and a current professional Ballroom Dance Instructor: Edward Phillip Moreno Pimentel!

Edward is the 4th GrandSon of Luis Pimentel Ruiz, and only offspring of Janet Pimentel Quiroga.

Even in her later years, Margarita occassionallly finds time to go to Muscle Beach and have some FUN ! ! ! !

Luis sends this letter to his 8 year-old son Francisco, who was still in Juarez as Luis made preparations to bring the family over to their new city! In the Letter, he tells Cisco that he is a good boy and to keep studying his math tables. He also told him that they would go fishing once they arrive, which are a few months away from when the letter was written!

In the letter, Luis still was a devote Catholic. However, religion became less important to him as time passed. He chose rather to spend the time doing acrobatics and having a positive mindset on things; rather than to have a religion dictate his life's journey! He found many hypocrisies in religion and thus chose another path of focus.

Below: Luis and Margarita Celebrating another anniversary together! JUNTOS!!!!

89

Left: Frances Rodriguez, Rosie's Only Daughter, pictured with Tito Gaona and Lee Ann MeriWether circa 1978. Tito was one of the most famous Trapeze artist of all time, having performed all over the World. He is from Guadalajara, Jalisco, Mexico whose circus roots date as far back as the late 1800's. The beautiful and kind Lee Ann MeriWether is a Los Angeles native who is an actress, model, a beauty pageant winner, amongst other accomplished activities she has been involved in.

Below: Luis still had his "Pulsador" wrist bands on at age 84. He took every opportunity if it presented itself for a possible hand-to-hand balancing moment.

Below Lft.: Cisco, Quinton "Rampage" Jackson, and Luis.

Quinton is from Memphis, Tennessee and is an actor, wrestler, mix-martial artist, among other endeavors he has pursued.

Above is a picture of one of Luis' brother Fermin Pimentel Ruiz. He had visited the couple in Juarez, but from there he disappeared and they never saw him again; although Luis attempted to find him and "El Zorro".

The *last person* Luis Pimentel ever held in his hands was **Mitch Gaylord**, the American Gold Medalist. Luis was 82 years old when he held Mitch at **Muscle Beach** in a low hand-to-hand balance, and then pushed him up to full arm extension.

Like all things in this world, there is a time limit (in preparation for something **better!! Yes!!!!!!!**).

Luis Pimentel Ruiz's body died on March 22, 2006 in Santa Monica, California of complications related to a cancer his body had contracted. Luis was 5 months shy of his 85th birthday when he moved on.

During his last days in this world, Luis Pimentel **always kept positive spirits and always kept a regimen of exercise to maintain the strength** his body had acquired through his devotion to the art of hand-balancing he held dear to his heart.

Luis learned from life to look beyond the difficulties he had as a child and the continual challenges life presented him. As such, **Luis Pimentel Ruiz** serves **TO THIS DAY** as a model of **perseverance and love**. He is missed. We will meet again! **Yes!!!***!!!* **Amen!!!**

Luis Pimentel Ruiz is a Victor! **VICTOR !!!**

CHAPTER 13 (1-pg. Chapter)
The Passion Continues---CHRIS PIMENTEL OROZCO
(Luis Pimentel's Gymnast Grandson!)

From all of the grandchildren of Luis Pimentel Ruiz, Francisco's youngest child, Christopher "Chris" Pimentel Orozco became the most enthusiastic and motivated in pursuing the art of acrobatics via the vehicle of Gymnastics.

At a tender 10 **Months** of age, Chris began to vividly show interest in acrobatics.

Francisco remembers that at those early moments of his life (10 **months!**), after Chris watched an acrobatic circus performance on the television set, Chris began trying to do a handstand on his mother's arm!!!!!

Another sign of interest came when Francisco was teaching Chris' older brother, Cisco Jr., who was age 6 at the time, to do a handstand against the wall. Chris immediately wanted to participate: at age 3 Chris immediately kicked his legs up and accomplished his first handstand against the wall!

In contrast to his older brother Cisco Jr., who began showing more interest in football and baseball instead of acrobatics, Chris showed immediate and continual interest in acrobatics! Acrobatics came "**natural**" for Chris (says his dad).

Chris' older sister, Diana Jr., did do gymnastics at an early age as well; but she decided to focus on other interests as well.

So at 4 ½ years of age, Chris' mother, Diana Pimentel Orozco, who has always been supportive of the culture of acrobatics, enrolled Chris into a gymnastics school. And from that moment on things developed for Chris in the world of acrobatics!

In the 2013 Men's Regional 1 Gymnastics Championship of the Southern California Men's Gymnastics Association, "Chis Pimentel Orozco" earned First Place in the All-Around Gymnastics Meet!

So at age 17, Chris in 2013, pursued something of value that requires tremendous amount of dedication **to perfect.**

So the saga of acrobatic enthusiasm established by Luis Pimentel Ruiz and Margarita Quiroga Torres de Pimentel continues to live on within the family!

CHAPTER FOURTEEN
EPILOGUE
Acrobatic Definition-Performance Evolution-Hand Balancing Techniques

The book has explored an incredible story of a man who loved the art of hand balancing...a derivative of acrobatics!

A brief history of acrobatic performance evolution and techniques for hand balancing will be explored in this last chapter as **a tribute to Luis Pimentel Ruiz**. A man who freely taught what he knew to those who were willing to learn!

Hopefully this epilogus chapter will help encourage those who would like to start off doing a bit of this art form that continues to this very day!

A Definition of Acrobatics

Acrobatics is a physical activity of the whole body where balance, motor skills, and agility are required to perform great bodily actions such as hand balancing, tumbling, jumping, contortions, and much more!

As to balance, the acrobat must equally distribute his or her weight or that of his or her partner(s) while performing movements such as tight-rope walking, hand balancing, hand-to-hand balancing of two or more participants!, and so on.

As to motor skills, the Acrobat must train his or her muscles to perform in ways that normally they would not do regularly: such as performing somersaults or pirouettes or hand balancing! A beginner in an art derivative of acrobatics trains his or her muscles so that "**muscle memory**" is achieved. This achieved muscle memory allows the Acrobat to repeat movements within the world of acrobatics **since now the muscle knows exactly how much energy is required** to stretch or contract during a particular movement; as well as **knowing the rate of the flexion/inflection of muscle tissue, and at what particular angles muscles are to place themselves in order to support** a particular movement or stance of the Acrobat.

By way of agility, the Acrobat moves quickly and gracefully from one position to another in his or her acrobatic movements. Such agility of an Acrobat comes with much practice by first training the muscles and working on maintaining balance in all sorts of physical artistic positions.

The word "acrobatics" comes from the Greek word akrobateō meaning to walk on tiptoe; denoting actions not normal in a human, but interesting to watch! Many times walking on tiptoe is mimicking an animal and the way it uses its feet to move its body.

Such mimicking of animals brings into focus the variations (derivatives) of acrobatics that are practiced. For example, the acrobatic art form of Ballet.

Ballet, as well as Diving, incorporates many aspects of acrobatics in executing its own acrobatic variation. In the world of Ballet, one sees athletes performing in half or full point of the toes or balls of the feet, mimicking an animal such as a deer. **The graceful steps of a danseur or ballerina** can also mimic such animals as cats or sea animals that continuously turn in the air with grace.

Gymnastics is another example of a derivative of acrobatics; it incorporates many forms of acrobatics that include Acro Dance, somersaults, the balancing of one's weight in many different types of positions and much more!

Tight-rope acrobatics is yet another derivative of acrobatics; it mimics birds on a branch or wire as they move easily across a narrow pathway! Hand balancers also mimic chimpanzees or other such animals.

The variations (derivatives) of acrobatics are open to the imagination; and much, but not all, of this imagination can be displayed in world competitions such as the Olympic Games, **and in circuses in every part of the world!!** *!!*

To name a few of the different derivatives of acrobatics that have opened themselves to our imagination!:

Hand Balancing, Hand-to-Hand Balancing, Acro Dance, Contortionism, Gymnastics (which encompasses many acrobatic movements), Ballet, Diving, Synchronized Swimming, Adagio Acrobatics, Tight-Rope Walking, Juggling, and Trapeze Art.

When one looks at any type of acrobatics, one normally sees a physically fit individual that has continuously practiced acrobatics **and thus trained the body to respond to the magical movements one sees Acrobats do!** Thus, for an Acrobat, **regular conditioning is required to keep him or herself physically fit (something demanded and necessary for the successful execution of any type of physical acrobatic art form)**, as well as to keep the muscles from forgetting to do what they have been trained to do by constant practice. As mentioned before in this book, **warming up the body before** any physical activity, especially an acrobatic one, **helps avoid physical injury!**

The Development of Acrobatics As Entertainment

The growing nourishment of acrobatics began via families that ran governments in civilizations such as those in Ancient Egypt, China, and Greece. Acrobatics began as a part of religious rituals and harvest celebrations as well as to catch prey or survive predator animals. Later within such cultures, it also began to be used as entertainment for the masses.

Into the future of thousands of years later, circuses began to use Acrobats to entertain their audiences. From the very first modern circuses started in England by Philip Astley (1742-1814) to the thousands of circuses that sprang up all over the world, acrobatics began to become more and more of a highlight to the overall circus show. The transition thus began to go from a dominance of equestrian acts to human acrobatic acts!

These circuses that came into being have come in many sizes, from very small to medium to large circuses. The well-known large circuses of modern times place acrobatics as prominence: such as the **Ringling Brother and Barnum and Bailey Circus** (1871 to 2017...and maybe returning 2023 but without animals) to the NOW famed Canadian **Cirque du Soleil.**

The Passing On of Acrobatic Skills

The process of teaching acrobatics from one generation to the next has traditionally been an endeavor from within families. That is, the passing on of acrobatic skills from parent to offspring. Dario Lucas, as shown in this book, is an example of this passing on of knowledge from parent to offspring.

However, such practice has been changing continuously as can be seen as to how **Luis Pimentel Ruiz learned acrobatics via joining a circus in the early 1940s.** The acrobatic families at the circus Luis entered were willing to share their acrobatic knowledge **to a non-family member** who showed an intense interest to learn their artistic acrobatical trade!

Today, the passing on of acrobatic skills is now also an endeavor of established institutions that teach non-family members the art of acrobatics. The famous Tito Gaona, the Flying Trapeze Legend, for example, has a school in Florida. And beyond that, there exists more and more such schools that have opened around the world: such as the **Moscow Circus School, the New York School for Circus Arts, the Ecole Nationale de Cirque** in Canada, the **Centre National des Arts du Cirque** in France, and the **Beijing International Arts School** in China to name a few! ...*a few!!!!!!!*

Hand Balancing Techniques

The following hand balancing information is not exhaustive or meant to lead the reader to a step by step approach in achieving hand balancing competence.

Rather, the objective here is to point out some important ingredients necessary for a successful hand balancing execution.

THE WALL

In my conversation with Dario Lucas, he mentioned that when he was very young, he learned how to do a handstand against a wall.

So an inclined person who wants to learn a handstand can do it against a wall or pole. Daily practice is important to begin to feel comfortable with being upside down and getting the entire body accustomed to the sudden change of direction of gravity exerted on the body.

Daily practice also helps strengthen the joints of the arms and hands for such an activity.

POSTURE

POSTURE is extremely important, if not **the most important aspect of any type of acrobatics.** And of course this is true for hand balancing. The body needs to be CONSISTENTLY aligned where the weight is evenly distributed in order to create equilibrium of balance while in a handstand. This too is practiced against the wall until it is achieved (this is reaffirmed as a good way to learn a handstand by Jarett Jamison, Dario Lucas, Lester James Lawton, and Luis Pimentel Ruiz).

What is Posture? ...the positioning of the whole body and or the limbs of the body (the arms and the legs). The word comes from the Latin verb "PONERE" which means to put or place. It was given a noun name of POSITURA. It is **the Mass Distribution of the body in a certain position according to the gravity that is imposed on it**.

The proper posture of an individual in any position is not the same from one person to the next. Although the bodies are built similar, variance in bone, muscle, ligaments, and tendon size and weight cannot pin point an exact angle or position for all bodies. **Humans are not physically created equal**; which makes **life interesting!:) J.**

However, the general rule of "good" posture can be found best by each individual conducting his or her **own reconnaissance** on his or herself! That is, one's own "good" posture is achieved by an individual **taking the time to explore his or her body and seeing how it best aligns itself to any particular position.** Thus, proper posture in a particular position is **achieved by taking the time of "doing"!!!!** The advice of practice, practice, practice is also taking into consideration the time to know one's own body well!

That is, achieve "**REFINED**" Proprioception by taking the time to know one's own body!

The degree of mastery of one's proper posture in different positions of one's body is thus one of **discovery!**

Handstand Variations

Variations of types of handstands are a matter of choice or type of executions intended to make while on a handstand.

Luis Pimentel Ruiz was taught a wide-arch approach as is seen in his early days photograph when he does one outside of a circus tent. Cisco and his friends preferred the "Gymnastic" style one of being vertical, straight up.

It appears that the wide-arch handstand allows for more stability and execution of contortions while in a handstand.

HEAD SHOULDER FEET

The author of this book remembers doing hand-to-hand balancing with **Luis Pimentel Ruiz** in his later years. One constant advice given was to always keep the head up, as if trying to look at the sky. This advice was given because of Luis' knowledge of a required posture: to stick one's chest out as far out as possible. This in turn obligates the "**shoulder in front**" of the arms; meaning, the shoulders should be slightly in front of the arms in order to achieve proper alignment for proper equilibrium of weight of the entire body while in a hand stand.

Feet should always be pointed while in a handstand as this helps the body by reminding the mind to stretch as much as possible as if one is being stretched. It also looks artistically better than feet that are dangling in different directions!!!!

"LOCKED" POSITION

Once stretched and once proper alignment are achieved, the body should be "locked" in position. Meaning, all the muscles connecting and holding all the bones, should be "stiff", fully contracted, wherein the bones maintain a fixed position (posture) while in a hand stand. This includes all the muscles that are around the body's multiple vertebra bones which come in different sizes and weight!!!

Being in a handstand requires "**grace**" in order for proper execution. Some beginner enthusiasts think they have this "grace" when they can run around on a walking handstand. However, this is cheating oneself since moving around in a handstand allows one to constantly find equilibrium of weight and make a quick adjustment if necessary. This mindset will not work in a hand STAND. "**Grace**" is required. And "**grace**" comes with practice that requires discipline and commitment.

LOCKING DURING HAND TO HAND BALANCING

When two or more people are involved in hand balancing, the bodies of the "base" and the "flyer", for example, **must be "locked" and in sync with one another.** When one moves slightly out of balance, the other must compensate and move toward repositioning in order to maintain balance.

KICKING UP OR PRESSING UP INTO A HANDSTAND

Kicking ones feet to get into a handstand is what is normally done in the beginning or in a situation that does not require "pressing". Kicking can either be with feet stretched or bent.

However, when one does a handstand on top of a person either in a hand-to-hand balancing situation or on the head in a one arm handstand or on some sort of instrument that can easily topple over, **"pressing"** into a handstand is required.

Pressing can be practiced against the wall in the same way one practices a handstand on the wall. The arms are slightly bent and the shoulders are in front of the arms as one leans forward and **slowly raises the hips above the shoulder.** Once the hips are fully stretched out where the back is vertically aligned with the coccyx area (the Gluteus Maximus area), **then the legs push up simultaneously as the arms extend fully**. The maneuver is **more about technique** rather than strength.

With sufficient practice, it becomes second nature. There are variations to this, such as the "planche" where one presses up with the legs straight at all times. However, this extension is more difficult for beginners and requires first learning to press up **with legs tucked in**.

Lester James commented that when you push up you **"push as if you're going through the ground"!** That is, **your whole body partakes in the full extension of the body as it unfolds itself** into a complete handstand position. **Lester James** says that with constant practice in the beginning the **necessary muscles begin to develop**: the development of muscle tissue and "muscle memory".

FINGERS AND LANDING

Lester James further elaborates that when you press up into a handstand **your fingers press down and act as "sensors" indicating not to go over too much in order to avoid tipping over.** Using only the palm of the hands will cause anyone to tip over. Therefore, the use of the fingers is a necessary ingredient.

When one returns to the ground from a handstand, the legs come down first slowly and then the buttocks bend forward for the landing!

WARM UP BEFORE YOUR ACROBATICAL ACTIVITY

In all exercises related to acrobatics, it is always a MUST to **thoroughly warm up the body by stretching BEFORE a work-out** in order to avoid injury (the tearing of muscle tissue or tendons or ligaments). The body must be aware that it is about to go into a workout that demands it to be ready and conditioned to go!!!! Depending on the weather, the warm up can be five to ten minutes. If in cold weather, the body will take longer to warm up and ready for action!!!!!!!

Good Days and Bad Days

Lester James commented that there are "good" days and "bad" days in doing hand-to-hand balancing. Sometimes everything is in sync and other times it is just not working out smoothly. When things are not moving as second nature, the participants have to **"muscle it through"** till completion.

After a "bad" endeavor of hand-to-hand balancing, it is always good to reflect and communicate with the other participant(s) as to what could have been done to make it better. **Communication is key in having less and less "bad" days.** So, daily practice is important, especially when working professionally. Many people think that when you go professional you practice less; the truth is opposite; daily practice is necessary to maintain bodily form and muscle memory so that when a public performance is presented, it is just like any other private rehearsal.

A Note as to a One-Arm Handstand

Learning to do a One-Arm Handstand comes with practice by first mastering a regular two arm handstand. Usually, one goes into a one arm handstand by first doing a two arm handstand. In the beginning, one practices a one arm handstand by slowly shifting the weight to one arm (in order to accustom the arm to the extra weight).

After a person has had sufficient practice with the weight, finding the correct position for the equal alignment of weight to achieve balance is practiced.

The **"locking"** of the arm is also critical as affirmed by both **Lester James Lawton and Dario Lucas**. The arm's shoulder goes into the truck of the body from where the joint begins, while at the same time stretching the arm as much as possible.

Once this is achieved, the "locking" is put into place where there is no more muscle movement as the arm becomes soldered, so to speak, with the trunk of the body. The other arm slowly rises and is placed where the hand slightly touches the front part of the femur.

95

Once the one-arm is accomplished and held, the return to two hands should be a slow transition. The landing is accomplished the same way as the two arm hand stand. If the one-arm handstand is on top of an object like a skull, then the return down should be the same as a two arm handstand with the exception that the one arm remains locked until the feet are completely planted firmly back on the ground or the shoulders of the "base" or the object that serves as the base.

Proper Nutrition

Eating healthy food is essential in maintaining a good Acrobatic Physique that can do what it is supposed to do when performing acrobatic feats. Good blood flow requires eating foods low in saturated fat; and the consumption amount should be less than the burning amount of calories. Otherwise, excess weight begins to build: making any task more difficult to accomplish.

Weight Lifting

Weight lifting does not mix well with acrobatics unless it is being built during the process of acrobatics. Excess muscles, as **Lester James** mentioned, gets in the way for the "locking" of the "base" and the "flyer" which is essential to a successful hand-to-hand balancing execution. Locking even within one's own body is also difficult to achieve with excess muscle.

Just as Lester James was told by Luis Pimentel Ruiz in Panama to lessen the weight lifting in order to achieve "locking" of bodies, so must any enthusiast who wishes to perfect any type of correct hand balancing alignment and locking. Ultimately, it is all about synchronization and locking that is achieved through "muscle memory". Every muscle in the body works uniformly to achieve synchronization in an acrobatic exercise!

FURTHER STUDY AND PLACE TO DO ACROBATICS

It is recommended that further study be achieved before attempting to do any acrobatic exercise since injury can be incurred if not properly informed of all the aspects related to an acrobatic execution of an exercise.

It is also recommended that the enthusiast find like-minded individuals to practice with since two or more minds are better than one! In Santa Monica, many people go to "Muscle Beach" to work out with others in doing the art of acrobatics. Meet up groups can also be organized by using many Online Meet Up Platforms.

Good luck and Best Wishes!

Sincerely,

David Darseli Santana

Right:
Maria Rosario Martinez Quiroga Torres in August of 1967, 3rd and Hill Street, Santa Monica, California.....
The Mother of the Author of This Book!

She is a native of Bogota, Colombia!

On an off note, a humanitarian organization is seeking to attempt to help mitigate human suffering. If you'd like to consider joining:

Eternoi.Com

Eternoi Humanitarian Organization (Eternoi)